The
Oxford Book
Of Canadian Verse

The
Oxford Book
Of Canadian Verse

Chosen by

Wilfred Campbell

GRANGER BOOKS
MIAMI, FLORIDA

First printed - 1913
Reprinted 1976

PREFACE

IN making this Anthology, I have endeavoured to cover the field of Canadian verse from the earliest colonial days down to the present time. It should be stated at the outset that the making of a collection of Canadian verse is no easy matter. It is extremely difficult to determine what, in the true sense of the word, may be called Canadian verse as distinguished from other verse of the same period.

Canada is not an old country covering centuries of development of one people and one language, like England or Scotland. It is a new region in the western world, where large numbers of the British peoples have, during the last century and a half, come and settled, transplanting their British ideals, traditions, religion, history, and heredity ; and their numbers, small at first, have been so often augmented or depleted from time to time, that it is very difficult to decide where to draw the line between what some might call the purely Canadian writer, and the writer who is a mere resident in Canada or born in Canada but living and writing elsewhere.

Another way in which to illustrate this peculiar

PREFACE

difficulty which faces the conscientious editor is to point out that our so-called Canadian literature (as claimed by many of our Anthologists and writers upon the subject) has been very inconsistently supposed to include the productions of the following four classes of writers :

First, those who, born in Canada, have written of Canada and upon other subjects.

Second, those who, though born in Canada, have lived in the United States and in other countries, and have there written the great bulk of their work and have identified themselves with the life of those countries, losing touch with Canada and its development.

Third, those who, though not born in Canada, have come to the country and have written about Canada.

Fourth, those who, coming to Canada in maturity, have written, while in the country, verse which has no relationship to the life of the country, and which might have been inspired by any other surroundings.

If this be a fair inclusion, a fifth class might more consistently be added, namely, those who, like Longfellow, Whittier, Goldsmith, and Moore, though never having lived in Canada, have written famous and distinctive poems like *Evangeline*, *Hiawatha*, and the *Death of Wolfe*, connected with the life, history, mythology, and natural environment of the country.

Here, at the outset, is a problem to be solved by the editor who aims at dealing in a proper manner

PREFACE

with our verse ; and a question for the sincere reader to face in his study of what is considered Canadian poetry.

It will be seen that former writers in their over-zealous efforts to claim as Canadian all versifiers who have been in any way at all connected with the country have been decidedly inconsistent, to say the least, in scooping all these classes of writers into their drag-net of colonial poetry.

Without doubt it must be acknowledged that the first class of writers mentioned, namely, those who, being born and having always lived in Canada, have written the large bulk of their work in the country, are the most decidedly Canadian, and have the first claim to such distinction. Only he who has been closely associated with a country from early childhood, and has spent all the years of his youth and maturity within its borders, can fitly interpret its life and dramatize its problems.

But this does not settle the question of the other classes referred to, which include many instances like that of Heavysege, an English dramatic writer, who came from England to Montreal when already in middle life, and soon after his arrival wrote some fine poetry and dramas, which have no more to do with Canada than they have to do with England, Scotland, or Ireland, save that they were written in Montreal.

The mere merit of Heavysege's work does not warrant us in considering him a Canadian writer.

PREFACE

But even if it did, what of several of our Canadian-born writers of verse, who have spent the greater part of their lives during the last quarter of a century in New York, Boston, and other American cities? We certainly cannot claim both classes; and yet this is just what has been attempted in a manner which is not only decidedly inconsistent, but is scarcely honest to Canadian and outside readers.

But there is another view to be taken of Canadian verse.

After all, the true British-Canadian verse, if it has any real root and lasting influence, must necessarily be but an offshoot of the great tree of British literature, as the American school also is, though less obviously. It might be said that all verse written in the English language, by persons of British heredity, must be of kin to the great continuity of verse from Chaucer, Shakespeare, and Milton down to the end of the eighteenth century.

What is purely Canadian in this offshoot of the parent stock must be decided, after all, by those canons which would constitute anything distinctly Canadian. But stronger even than the so-called Canadian spirit is the voice of the Vaster Britain, which finds its utterance in the works of her poets.

It is this consideration which has led me to include a number of poems by the Duke of Argyll, Governor-General of Canada from 1878 to 1883. To claim him as a Canadian poet would clearly be an exaggeration;

PREFACE

but his verse is so inspired by the country, which was his home for five years, and his position lends it such a peculiar interest, that I have ventured, in this instance, to break the stricter canons.

The spirit of true poetry will always rise beyond what is merely local, and one of its greatest influences on mankind is its constant demand for that wider horizon, that larger outlook, which would recall man, dwarfed by materialism, to the greater, vaster, and more universal environment which he inherits in this wide domain of nature, as spiritual lord and trustee of the planet on which he dwells.

As for this collection, it does not pretend to do justice to the work of the poets of Canada, a thing which it would be impossible to accomplish in any single volume. A poet who has devoted years to his vocation can only be appreciated through a perusal of the whole of his work ; and no anthology can claim either to do justice to the literature of a country or the work of a single writer. This volume is rather a collection of short poems culled from the verse of Canadian writers, and covering in its range the century and a half of time between the capture of Quebec and the present day. The editor has striven to do justice to the earlier periods of the life of the country, with the result that there are selections of verse in this volume which now appear for the first time in the pages of any Canadian anthology.

This is not only necessary in order to do justice to

PREFACE

our earlier verse-writers, but to give a proper view of the gradual development of our verse. Too much in the past has been made of the work of our later, more brilliant groups of versifiers who distinguished the last decade of the nineteenth century, with the result that our earlier writers have been sadly neglected —a result which Professor Horning, one of our ablest critics, was the first to deplore. A proper study of the work done prior to and immediately following Confederation, will show that verse worthy of any anthology was to be found in the pages of the *Literary Garland* in 1840, and reveal the fine poetic excellence of such writers as Sangster and Mair, the latter of whom was the real founder of the Canadian classical-nature school of verse.

The verse of French Canada has no proper place in this collection. It is written in the French language, and is as much an offshoot of French literature as the literature of British Canada is of that of Britain. Its poets naturally look altogether to Paris for their ideals, recognition, and encouragement. Several of them have been honoured by decorations from the French Government, and recognition by the French Academy, though Frechette, the most distinguished during the nineteenth century, was granted the Companionship of the Order of St. Michael and St. George by the British Government.

Whatever may be the reader's opinion regarding the value of such a collection as this, the editor at least

PREFACE

hopes that it may give English readers throughout the world a renewed interest in what has been called Canadian poetry.

The editor's thanks are due to the following, as authors, representatives, trustees, or publishers, for permission to use copyright poems : Miss Murray, Mrs. Davin, Mrs. Drummond, Miss Machar, Miss Wetherald, Mrs. Blewett, Miss Johnson, Miss McManus, Miss Graham, Mrs. Garvin,—' Katherine Hale ', Miss Merrill, Miss Coleman, Miss Pickthall, Mrs. M. B. Grey, Mr. J. J. McGee, Mr. Colin A. Scott, the Trustees of the Lampman Estate, Mr. J. O. Clarke, Mr. Arthur L. Phelps, Mr. John Reade, the Duke of Argyll, Mr. Charles Mair, Mr. E. W. Thomson, Mr. W. D. Lighthall, Mr. C. G. D. Roberts, Mr. Bliss Carman, the Rev. Canon Scott, Mr. D. C. Scott, Mr. J. E. Caldwell, Mr. Arthur Stringer, Mr. Peter McArthur, the Rev. Archdeacon Armitage; and to the William Briggs Publishing House for the poems from the works of Robert W. Service, Alexander McLachlan, and J. S. Thomson.

His thanks are also due for permission to include copyright poems by the following authors : Messrs. William T. Allison, John K. Bathurst, John H. Brown, Hector Charlesworth, A. F. Bruce Clark, J. C. M. Duncan, Alexander L. Fraser, Charles A. Lazenby, John Daniel Logan, Peter M. Macdonald, George A. MacKenzie, Newton MacTavish, William E. Marshall,

PREFACE

J. Edgar Middleton, Theodore Roberts, William C.
Roberts, Richard Scrace, Virna Sheard, Francis
Sherman, Albert E. S. Smythe, Alan Sullivan, Archibald Sullivan, Albert D. Watson, W. Stewart Wallace,
and Eric M. Yeoman.

BISHOP G. J. MOUNTAIN

1.   *The Indian's Grave*

BRIGHT are the heavens, the narrow bay serene ;
   No sound is heard within the shelter'd place,
Save some sweet whisper of the pines—nor seen
   Of restless man, nor of his works, a trace ;
   I stray, through bushes low, a little space ;
Unlook'd-for sight their parted leaves disclose :
   Restless no more, lo ! one of Indian race,
His bones beneath that roof of bark repose.

Poor savage ! in such bark through deepening snows
   Once didst thou dwell ; in this through rivers move.
Frail house, frail skiff, frail man ! Of him who knows
   His master's will, not thine the doom shall prove.
What will be yours, ye powerful, wealthy, wise,
By whom the heathen unregarded dies ?

SUSANNA MOODIE

2.   *Indian Summer*

BY the purple haze that lies
   On the distant rocky height,
By the deep blue of the skies,
   By the smoky amber light

SUSANNA MOODIE

Through the forest arches streaming,
Where Nature on her throne sits dreaming,
And the sun is scarcely gleaming
  Through the cloudlets, snowy white,
Winter's lovely herald greets us
Ere the ice-crowned tyrant meets us.

A mellow softness fills the air,
  No breeze on wanton wing steals by
To break the holy quiet there,
  Or make the waters fret and sigh,
Or the golden alders shiver
That bend to kiss the placid river,
Flowing on and on for ever.
But the little waves are sleeping,
O'er the pebbles slowly creeping,
That last night were flashing, leaping,
Driven by the restless breeze,
In lines of foam beneath yon trees.

Dressed in robes of gorgeous hue,
  Brown and gold with crimson blent ;
The forest to the waters blue
  Its own enchanting tints has lent ;
In their dark depths, life-like glowing,
We see a second forest growing,
Each pictured leaf and branch bestowing
A fairy grace to that twin wood,
Mirror'd within the crystal flood.

2

SUSANNA MOODIE

'Tis pleasant now in forest shades ;
   The Indian hunter strings his bow
To track through dark, entangling glades
   The antler'd deer and bounding doe,
Or launch at night the birch canoe,
To spear the finny tribes that dwell
On sandy bank, in weedy cell,
Or pool the fisher knows right well—
Seen by the red and vivid glow
Of pine-torch at his vessel's bow.

This dreamy Indian-summer day
   Attunes the soul to tender sadness ;
We love—but joy not in the ray :
   It is not summer's fervid gladness,
But a melancholy glory
   Hovering softly round decay,
Like swan that sings her own sad story
   Ere she floats in death away

The day declines ; what splendid dyes,
   In flickered waves of crimson driven,
Float o'er the saffron sea that lies
   Glowing within the western heaven !
   Oh, it is a peerless even !
See, the broad red sun is set,
But his rays are quivering yet
Through nature's veil of violet,
Streaming bright o'er lake and hill ;

But earth and forest lie so still,
It sendeth to the heart a chill;
We start to check the rising tear—
'Tis Beauty sleeping on her bier.

3.   *The Canadian Herd-boy*

(A SONG OF THE BACKWOODS)

THROUGH the deep woods, at peep of day,
The careless herd-boy wends his way,
By piny ridge and forest stream,
To summon home his roving team :
Cobos ! Cobos ! from distant dell
Sly echo wafts the cattle-bell.

A blithe reply he whistles back,
And follows out the devious track,
O'er fallen tree and mossy stone,
A path to all save him unknown :
Cobos ! Cobos ! far down the dell
More faintly falls the cattle-bell.

See, the dark swamp before him throws
A tangled maze of cedar boughs;
On all around deep silence broods
In Nature's boundless solitudes:
Cobos ! Cobos ! the breezes swell
As nearer floats the cattle-bell.

4

SUSANNA MOODIE

He sees them now ; beneath yon trees
His motley herd recline at ease ;
With lazy pace and sullen stare
They slowly leave their shady lair :
Cobos ! Cobos ! far up the dell
Quick jingling comes the cattle-bell.

ELIZABETH L. CUSHING

4. *April*

HARK to the silvery sound
    Of the soft April shower !
Telleth it not a pleasant tale
    Of bird and bee and flower ?
See, as the bright drops fall,
    How swell the tiny buds
That gem each bare and leafless bough
    Like polished agate studs.

The alder by the brook
    Stands in her tasselled pride ;
Oh, the pale willow decketh her
    As might beseem a bride;
And round the old oak's foot,
    Where in their wintry play
The winds have swept the withered leaves,
    See, the Hepatica !

5

ELIZABETH L. CUSHING

Its brown and mossy buds
　　Greet the first breath of Spring;
And to her shrine its clustered flowers
　　Their earliest offering bring.
In rocky cleft secure,
　　The gaudy columbine
Shoots forth, ere wintry snows have fled,
　　A floral wreath to twine.

And many a bud lies hid
　　Beneath the foliage sere,
Waiting spring's warm and wooing breath
　　To deck the vernal year,
When, lo! sweet April comes—
　　The wild bird hears her voice,
And through the groves on glancing wing
　　Carols, 'Rejoice! rejoice!'

Forth from her earthy nest
　　The timid wood-moose steals,
And the blithe squirrel on the bough
　　Her genial influence feels.
The purple hue of life
　　Flushes the teeming earth;
Above, around, beneath the feet,
　　Joy, beauty, spring to birth.

But on the distant verge
　　Of the cerulean sky
Old Winter stands with angry frown
　　And bids the siren fly.

6

ELIZABETH L. CUSHING

He waves his banner dark,
  Raises his icy hand,
And the fierce storms of sleet and hail
  Obey his grim command.

She feareth not his wrath,
  But hides her sunny face
Behind a soft cloud's fleecy fold
  For a brief instant's space ;
Then looketh gaily forth
  With smile of magic power,
That changeth all his icy darts
  To a bright diamond shower.

Capricious April, hail !
  Herald of all things fair !
'Tis thine to loose the imprisoned streams,
  The young buds are thy care.
To unobservant eye
  Thy charms are few, I ween ;
But he who roves the woodland paths
  Where thy blithe foot hath been,

Will trace thee by the tufts
  Of fragrant early flowers,
That thy sweet breath hath waked to deck
  The dreary forest bowers ;
And by the bursting buds,
  That at thy touch unfold
To clothe the tall trees' naked arms
  With beauty all untold ;

7

Will hear thy tuneful voice
In the glad leaping streams,
And catch thy bland, yet fitful smile
In showers and sunny gleams ;—
Then welcome, April fair,
Bright harbinger of May,
Month of blue skies and perfumed airs—
The young year's holiday !

5.   *The City Elms*

OLD trees, I love your shade,
Though not on banks with wild flowers all
bedight
Falls through your trembling boughs the chequered
light,
As in some forest glade
Where woos the murmuring bee.

Yet, ye to me do bring
Thoughts of the breezy hill, the free green wood,
The gushing stream that over fragments rude
Its silvery foam doth fling,
In wild fantastic play.

There 's music in the sound,
O verdant elms ! of your green whispering leaves.
Music my spirit loves, and yet it grieves
That ye should here be found,
Soiled with the city's dust.
8

ELIZABETH L. CUSHING

Here, amid pent-up streets,
Where never the glad tones of Nature's voice
Steal in to soothe the harsh discordant noise,
The wearied ear that greets
With ceaseless jar and din.

Here, rude hands have marred
Your stately forms and uncouth objects piled
Around your trunks, where should have gaily smiled
Banks with the primrose starred,
Or bright anemone.

Yet, yet to me ye are
A joy and a delight for ever new ,
Lovely to sense and thought is your soft hue,
Or e'en your branches bare
When Winter rules the year.

E. T. F.

(A lady living in Quebec, 1840)

6.   *Lilith*

THERE was a broad, still lake near Paradise,
A lake, where silence rested evermore ;
And yet not gloomy, for along the shore
Majestic trees and flowers of deepest dyes
Drunk the rich light of those unclouded skies ;

E. T. F.

But noiseless all. By night the moonshine hoar
And stars in alternating companies ;
By day the sun ; no other change it wore.
And hither came the sire of men and stood
Breathless amid the breathless solitude.
He plunged ; the waters muttered where he fell.
He entered a cavern dim ; how wonderful !
High-arched above, and water-paved below.
Pale phosphor cressets with a wavering glow
Lit up the mighty vault. A whisper cool
Ran muttering all around him, and a dull
Sweet sound of music drifted to and fro,
Wordless, yet full of thought unspeakable,
Till all the place was teeming with its flow.
' Adam ! strong child of light ! ' Who calls ? who
    speaks ?
What voice, mysterious, the silence breaks.
Is it a vision or reality ?
How marble-like her face ! How pale her cheeks !
Yet fair, and in her glorious stature high
Above the daughters of mortality.
And this was Lilith. And she came to him,
And looked into him with her dreamy eyes,
Till all his former life seemed old and dim,
A thing that had been once ; and Paradise,
Its antique forests, floods, and choral skies,
Now faded quite away ; or seemed to skim,
Like eagles on a bright horizon's rim,
Darkly across his golden phantasies.

And he forgot the sunshine and sweet flowers,
And he forgot all pleasant things that be,
The birds of Eden, and the wingèd powers
That visited sometime its privacy;
And what to him was day or day-lit hours,
Or the moon shining on an open sea !

JOSEPH HOWE

7.   *Our Fathers*

ROOM for the dead ! Your living hands may pile
    Treasures of art the stately tents within,
Beauty may grace them with her richest smile,
    And genius there spontaneous plaudits win :
But yet amidst the tumult and the din
    Of gathering thousands, let me audience crave !
Place claim I for the Dead—'twere mortal sin,
    When banners o'er our country's treasures wave,
    Unmarked to leave the wealth, safe garnered in the
        grave.

The fields may furnish forth their lowing kine,
    The forest spoils in rich abundance lie,
The mellow fruitage of the clustered vine
    Mingle with flowers of every varied dye ;
Swart artisans their rival skill may try,
    And while the rhetorician wins the ear,
The pencil's graceful shadows charm the eye ;
    But yet, do not withhold the grateful tear
    For those, and for their works, who are not here.

JOSEPH HOWE

Not here ?   O yes ! our hearts their presence feel,
  Viewless, not voiceless ; from the deepest shells
On memory's shore harmonious echoes steal,
  And names which in the days gone by were spells
Are blent with that soft music.   If there dwells
  The spirit here our country's fame to spread,
While every breast with joy and triumph swells,
  And earth reverberates to our measured tread,
  Banner and wreath will own our reverence for the
    Dead.

Look up ! their walls enclose us.   Look around !
  Who won the verdant meadows from the sea ?
Whose sturdy hands the noble highways wound
  Through forest dense, o'er mountain, moor, and lea ?
Who spanned the streams ?   Tell me, whose work
    they be,
  The busy marts where commerce ebbs and flows ?
Who quelled the savage ?   And who spared the tree
  That pleasant shelter o'er the pathway throws ?
  Who made the land they loved to blossom as the rose ?

Who, in frail barks, the ocean surge defied,
  And trained the race that live upon the wave ?
What shore so distant where they have not died ?
  In every sea they found a watery grave.
Honour for ever to the true and brave,
  Who seaward led their sons with spirits high,
Bearing the red-cross flag their fathers gave ;
  Long as the billows flout the arching sky,
  They'll seaward bear it still—to venture or to die.

JOSEPH HOWE

The Roman gathered in a stately urn
   The dust he honoured, while the sacred fire,
Nourished by vestal hands, was made to burn
   From age to age. If fitly you'ld aspire,
Honour the Dead ; and let the sounding lyre
   Recount their virtues in your festal hours.
Gather their ashes ; higher still, and higher
   Nourish the patriot flame that history dowers,
   And o'er the old men's graves go strew your choicest
     flowers.

C. D. SHANLY

8.   *The Walker of the Snow*

SPEED on, speed on, good Master !
   The camp lies far away ;
We must cross the haunted valley
   Before the close of day.

How the snow-blight came upon me
   I will tell you as we go,
The blight of the Shadow Hunter
   Who walks the midnight snow.

To the cold December heaven
   Came the pale moon and the stars,
As the yellow sun was sinking
   Behind the purple bars.

C. D. SHANLY

The snow was deeply drifted
  Upon the ridges drear
That lay for miles between me
  And the camp for which we steer.

'Twas silent on the hill-side
  And by the sombre wood,
No sound of life or motion
  To break the solitude,

Save the wailing of the moose-bird
  With a plaintive note and low,
And the skating of the red leaf
  Upon the frozen snow.

And I said, ' Though dark is falling
  And far the camp must be,
Yet my heart it would be lightsome
  If I had but company.'

And then I sang and shouted,
  Keeping measure as I sped,
To the harp-twang of the snowshoe
  As it sprang beneath my tread.

Nor far into the valley
  Had I dipped upon my way
When a dusky figure joined me,
  In a capuchon of grey,

C. D. SHANLY

Bending upon the snowshoes
  With a long and limber stride ;
And I hailed the dusky stranger
  As we travelled side by side.

But no token of communion
  Gave he by word or look,
And the fear-chill fell upon me
  At the crossing of the brook.

For I saw by the sickly moonlight,
  As I followed, bending low,
That the walking of the stranger
  Left no footmarks on the snow.

Then the fear-chill gathered o'er me
  Like a shroud around me cast,
As I sank upon the snow-drift
  Where the Shadow Hunter passed.

And the otter-trappers found me
  Before the break of day,
With my dark hair blanched and whitened
  As the snow in which I lay.

But they spoke not as they raised me ;
  For they knew that in the night
I had seen the Shadow Hunter,
  And had withered in his blight.

15

Sancta Maria, speed us !
The sun is falling low ;
Before us lies the valley
Of the Walker of the Snow !

JAMES McCARROLL

9.   *Dawn*

WITH folded wings of dusky light
    Upon the purple hills she stands,
An angel between day and night,
    With tinted shadows in her hands ;

Till suddenly transfigured there,
    With all her dazzling plumes unfurled
She climbs the crimson-flooded air,
    And flies in glory o'er the world.

10.   *The Grey Linnet*

THERE 'S a little grey friar in yonder green bush,
    Clothed in sackcloth—a little grey friar,
Like a druid of old in his temple—but hush !
    He 's at vespers ; you must not go nigher.

16

JAMES McCARROLL

Yet, the rogue ! can those strains be addressed to the
  skies,
  And around us so wantonly float,
Till the glowing refrain like a shining thread flies
  From the silvery reel of his throat ?

When he roves, though he stains not his path through
  the air
  With the splendour of tropical wings,
All the lustre denied to his russet plumes there
  Flashes forth through his lay when he sings.

For the little grey friar is so wondrous wise,
  Though in such a plain garb he appears,
That on finding he can't reach your soul through your
  eyes
  He steals in through the gates of your ears.

But—the cheat !—'tis not heaven he 's warbling about.
  Other passions, less holy, betide.
For behold ! there 's a little grey nun peeping out
  From a bunch of green leaves at his side.

CHARLES HEAVYSEGE

11.   *Winter Night*

THE stars are glittering in the frosty sky,
    Numerous as pebbles on a broad sea-coast ;
While o'er the vault the cloud-like galaxy
    Has marshalled its innumerable host.
Alive all heaven seems ; with wondrous glow
    Tenfold refulgent every star appears ;
As if some wide, celestial gale did blow,
    And thrice illume the ever-kindled spheres.

Orbs, with glad orbs rejoicing, burning, beam,
    Ray-crowned, with lambent lustre in their zones ;
Till o'er the blue, bespangled spaces seem
    Angels and great archangels on their thrones ;
A host divine, whose eyes are sparkling gems,
And forms more bright than diamond diadems.

12.   *Self-Examination*

OPEN, my heart, thy ruddy valves ;
    It is thy master calls ;
Let me go down and, curious, trace
    Thy labyrinthine halls.
Open, O heart, and let me view
    The secrets of thy den ;
My self unto myself now show
    With introspective ken.

18

Expose thyself, thou covered nest
  Of passions, and be seen ;
Stir up thy brood, that in unrest
  Are ever piping keen.
Ah ! what a motley multitude,
  Magnanimous and mean !

13.   *Night*

'TIS solemn darkness ; the sublime of shade ;
  Night by no stars nor rising moon relieved ;
The awful blank of nothingness arrayed,
  O'er which my eyeballs roll in vain, deceived.
Upward, around, and downward I explore,
  E'en to the frontiers of the ebon air,
But cannot, though I strive, discover more
  Than what seems one huge cavern of despair.
O Night, art thou so grim, when black and bare
  Of moonbeams, and no cloudlets to adorn ?
Like a nude Ethiop 'twixt two houris fair
  Thou standest between the evening and the morn.
I took thee for an angel, but have wooed
A cacodaemon in mine ignorant mood.

14.   *The Scot abroad*

OH, to be in Scotland now,
    When the yellow autumn smiles
So pleasantly on knoll and how ;
Where from rugged cliff and heathy brow
    Of each mountain height you look down defiles
Golden with the harvest's glow.

Oh, to be in the kindly land,
    Whether mellow autumn smiles or no.
It is well if the joyous reaper stand
Breast-deep in the yellow corn, sickle in hand ;
    But I care not though sleety east winds blow,
So long as I tread its strand.

To be wandering there at will,
    Be it sunshine or rain, or its winds that brace ;
To climb the old familiar hill ;
Of the storied landscape to drink my fill,
    And look out on the grey old town at its base,
And linger a dreamer still.

Ah ! weep ye not for the dead,
    The dear ones safe in their native earth ;
There fond hands pillowed the narrow bed
Where fresh gowans, starlike, above their head
    Spangle the turf of each spring's new birth
For the living, loving tread.
    20

SIR DANIEL WILSON

Ah ! not for them ; doubly blest,
  Safely home, and past all weeping ;
Hushed and still, there closely pressed
Kith to kin on one mother's breast
  All still, securely, trustfully sleeping,
As in their first cradled rest.

Weep rather, aye, weep sore,
  For him who departs to a distant land.
There are pleasant homes on the far-off shore ;
Friends too, but not like the friends of yore
  That fondly, but vainly, beckoning stand
For him who returns no more.

Oh, to lie in Scottish earth,
  Lapped in the clods of its kindly soil ;
Where the soaring laverock's song has birth
In the welkin's blue, and its heavenward mirth
  Lends a rapture to earth-born toil—
What matter ! Death recks not the dearth.

SIR J. H. HAGARTY

15.   *Funeral of Napoleon I*
              (*Dec. 15, 1840*)

COLD and brilliant streams the sunlight on the
     wintry banks of Seine ;
Gloriously the imperial city rears her pride of tower
     and fane ;

SIR J. H. HAGARTY

Solemnly with deep voice pealeth Nôtre Dame, thine
    ancient chime ;
Minute-guns the death-bell answer in the same deep,
    measured time.

On the unwonted stillness gather sounds of an advanc-
    ing host,
As the rising tempest chafeth on St. Helen's far-off
    coast ;
Nearer rolls a mighty pageant, clearer swells the funeral
    strain ;
From the barrier arch of Neuilly pours the giant burial
    train.

Dark with eagles is the sunlight, darkly on the golden
    air
Flap the folds of faded standards, eloquently mourning
    there ;
O'er the pomp of glittering thousands, like a battle-
    phantom flits
Tatter'd flag of Jena, Friedland, Arcola, and Austerlitz.

Eagle-crown'd and garland-circled, slowly moves the
    stately car
'Mid a sea of plumes and horsemen, all the burial
    pomp of war.
Riderless, a war-worn charger follows his dead master's
    bier ;
Long since battle-trumpet roused him, he but lived
    to follow here.

SIR J. H. HAGARTY

From his grave 'mid Ocean's dirges, moaning surge
    and sparkling foam,
Lo, the Imperial Dead returneth! lo, the Hero dust
    comes home!
He hath left the Atlantic island, lonely vale and
    willow-tree,
'Neath the Invalides to slumber, 'mid the Gallic
    chivalry.

Glorious tomb o'er glorious sleepers! gallant fellow-
    ship to share—
Paladin and peer and marshal—France, thy noblest
    dust is there!
Names that light thy battle annals, names that shook
    the heart of earth!
Stars in crimson War's horizon—synonyms for martial
    worth!

Room within that shrine of heroes! place, pale spectres
    of the past!
Homage yield, ye battle-phantoms. Lo, your
    mightiest comes at last!
Was his course the Woe out-thunder'd from prophetic
    trumpet's lips?
Was his type the ghostly horseman shadow'd in the
    Apocalypse?

Grey-hair'd soldiers gather round him, relics of an age
    of war,
Followers of the Victor-Eagle, when his flight was wild
    and far.

Men who panted in the death-strife on Rodrigo's
    bloody ridge,
Hearts that sicken'd at the death-shriek from the
    Russian's shatter'd bridge ;

Men who heard the immortal war-cry of the wild
    Egyptian fight—
' Forty centuries o'erlook us from yon Pyramid's grey
    height ! '
They who heard the moans of Jaffa, and the breach
    of Acre knew,
They who rushed their foaming war-steeds on the
    squares of Waterloo ;

They who loved him, they who fear'd him, they who
    in his dark hour fled,
Round the mighty burial gather, spellbound by the
    awful Dead !
Churchmen, princes, statesmen, warriors, all a king-
    dom's chief array,
And the Fox stands, crownèd mourner, by the Eagle's
    hero clay !

But the last high rite is paid him, and the last deep
    knell is rung,
And the cannons' iron voices have their thunder-
    requiem sung ;
And, 'mid banners idly drooping, silent gloom and
    mouldering state,
Shall the trampler of the world upon the Judgement-
    trumpet wait.

Yet his ancient foes had given him nobler monumental
    pile,
Where the everlasting dirges moan'd around the burial
    isle ;
Pyramid upheaved by Ocean in his loneliest wilds afar,
For the War-King thunder-stricken from his fiery
    battle-car !

16.   *The Sea*

THE sea ! the sea !
    For the light of thy waves we bless thee :
  For the foam on thine ancient brow ;
For the winds, whose bold wings caress thee,
  Old Ocean ! we bless thee now !
Oh, welcome thy long-lost minstrelsy ;
Thy thousand voices ; the wild, the free,
The fresh, cool breeze o'er thy sparkling breast ;
The sunlit foam on each billow's crest,
Thy joyous rush up the sounding shore,
Thy song of Freedom for evermore,
And thy glad waves shouting, ' Rejoice ! Rejoice ! '
Old Ocean ! welcome thy glorious voice !

        The sea ! the sea !
We bless thee ; we bless thee, Ocean !
  Bright goal of our weary track,
With the exile's rapt devotion,
  To the home of his love come back.

25

SIR J. H. HAGARTY

When gloom lay deep on our fainting hearts,
When the air was dark with the Persian darts,
When the desert rung with the ceaseless war,
And the wish'd-for fountain and palm afar,
In Memory's dreaming, in Fancy's ear,
The chime of thy joyous waves was near,
And the last fond prayer of each troubled night
Was for thee and thine islands of love and light.

The sea ! the sea !
Sing on thy majestic paean ;
    Leap up in the Delian's smiles ;
We will dream of the blue Aegean,
    Of the breath of Ionia's isles ;
Of the hunter's shout through the Thracian woods ;
Of the shepherd's song by the Dorian floods ;
Of the naiad springing by Attic fount ;
Of the satyrs' dance by the Cretan mount ;
Of the sun-bright gardens, the bending vines,
Our virgins' songs by the flower-hung shrines ;
Of the dread Olympian's majestic domes,
Our father's graves and our own free homes.

The sea ! the sea !
We bless thee, we bless thee, Ocean !
    Bright goal of our stormy track,
With the exile's rapt devotion,
    To the home of his love come back.

ALEXANDER McLACHLAN

17.   *May*

THE cataract's horn
    Has awakened the morn,
Her tresses are dripping with dew ;
    Oh, hush thee and hark !
    'Tis her herald the lark
That is singing afar in the blue :
    Its happy heart 's rushing,
    In strains mildly gushing,
That reach to the revelling earth,
    And sink through the deeps
    Of the soul, till it leaps
Into raptures far deeper than mirth.

    All Nature 's in keeping,
    The live streams are leaping,
And laughing in gladness along ;
    The great hills are heaving,
    The dark clouds are leaving,
The val'eys have burst into song.
    We'll range through the dells
    Of the bonnie blue-bells,
And sing with the streams on their way ;
    We'll lie in the shades
    Of the flower-covered glades,
And hear what the primroses say.

Oh, crown me with flowers
'Neath the green spreading bowers,
With the gems and the jewels May brings ;
    In the light of her eyes,
    And the depth of her dyes,
We'll smile at the purple of kings !
    We'll throw off our years,
    With their sorrows and tears,
And time will not number the hours
    We'll spend in the woods,
    Where no sorrow intrudes,
With the streams, and the birds, and the flowers.

18.   *Old Hannah*

'TIS Sabbath morn, and a holy balm
    Drops down on the heart like dew,
And the sunbeams gleam like a blessèd dream,
    Afar on the mountains blue.
Old Hannah's by her cottage door
    In her faded widow's cap ;
She is sitting alone on the old grey stone,
    With the Bible in her lap.

An oak is hanging above her head,
    And the burn is wimpling by ;
The primroses peep from their sylvan keep,
    And the lark is in the sky.

28

ALEXANDER McLACHLAN

Beneath that shade her children played,
    But they're all away with Death,
And she sits alone on the old grey stone
    To hear what the Spirit saith.

Her years are past three score and ten,
    And her eyes are waxing dim,
But the page is bright with a living light,
    And her heart leaps up to Him
Who pours the mystic Harmony
    Which the soul alone can hear !
She is not alone on the old grey stone,
    Though no earthly friend is near.

There 's no one left to love her now ;
    But the Eye that never sleeps
Looks on her in love from the heavens above,
    And with quiet joy she weeps.
For she feels the balm of bliss is poured
    In her lone heart's sorest spot :
The widow lone on the old grey stone
    Has a peace the world knows not.

REV. R. J. McGEORGE

19.   *The Emigrant's Funeral*

STRANGE earth we sprinkle on the exile's clay,
    Mingled with flowers his childhood never knew ;
Far sleeps he from that mountain-top so blue,
    Shadowing the scene of his young boyhood's play.
But o'er his lonely transatlantic bed
    The ancient words of hopeful love are spoken ;
    The solitude of these old pines is broken
With the same prayers once o'er his father said.

O precious Liturgy ! that thus canst bring
    Such sweet associations to the soul,
    That though between us and our homes seas roll,
We oft in thee forget our wandering,
And in a holy day-dream tread once more
The fresh green valleys of our native shore.

E. J. CHAPMAN

20.   *A Question*

Prologue to ' The Drama of Two Lives '

ART thou the old dream dreaming ?
    Poor heart, of the morrow beware !
Death may lurk in the brown eyes' veiled gleaming,
    In the white throat so wondrously fair.

E. J. CHAPMAN

The tones that wild heart-throbs awaken,
  The sheen of the gold-showered hair,
The touch that thy soul hath so shaken
  May lure thee and leave thee—ah, where ?

Trust it not, the wild, treacherous gladness :
  The twin hounds of passion and pain
Are swift to arise in their madness
  They rend, and they rest not again !
The day-dream is sweet in the dreaming,
  But dreamless the night's dull despair,
When the voice and the touch and the gleaming
  Have lured thee, and left thee—ah, where ?

CHARLES SANGSTER

21.   *Brock*

O NE voice, one people, one in heart,
  And soul, and feeling, and desire.
    Re-light the smouldering martial fire,
    And sound the mute trumpet ! Strike the lyre !
    The hero dead cannot expire ;
  The dead still play their part.

Raise high the monumental stone !
    A nation's fealty is theirs ;
    And we are the rejoicing heirs,
    The honoured sons of sires, whose cares ·
    We take upon us unawares
  As freely as our own.

31

CHARLES SANGSTER

We boast not of the victory,
   But render homage, deep and just,
   To his—to their—immortal dust,
   Who proved so worthy of their trust ;
   No lofty pile nor sculptured bust
Can herald their degree.

No tongue can blazon forth their fame—
   The cheers that stir the sacred hill
   Are but mere promptings of the will
   That conquered them, that conquers still ;
   And generations yet shall thrill
At Brock's remembered name.

Some souls are the Hesperides
   Heaven sends to guard the golden age,
   Illuming the historic page
   With record of their pilgrimage ;
   True martyr, hero, poet, sage ;—
And he was one of these.

Each in his lofty sphere, sublime,
   Sits crowned above the common throng ;
   Wrestling with some pythonic wrong
   In prayer, in thunders, thought or song,
   Briareus-limbed, they sweep along,
The Typhons of the time.

CHARLES SANGSTER

22. *Evening*

ONE solitary bird melodiously
    Trilled its sweet vesper from a grove of elm,
One solitary sail upon the sea
    Rested, unmindful of its potent helm.

And down behind the forest trees the sun,
    Arrayed in burning splendours, slowly rolled,
Like to some sacrificial urn, o'errun
    With flaming hues of crimson, blue and gold.

The fisher ceased his song, hung on his oars,
    Pausing to look, a pulse in every breath,
And, in imagination, saw the shores
    Elysian, rising o'er the realms of Death.

And down on tiptoe came the gradual night,
    A gentle twilight first, with silver wings,
And still from out the darkening infinite
    Came shadowy forms, like deep imaginings.

There was no light in all the brooding air,
    There was no darkness yet to blind the eyes,
But through the space interminable, there
    Nature and Silence passed in solemn guise.

CHARLES SANGSTER

23.   *A Northern Rune*

L OUD rolleth the rune, the martial rune
    Of the Norse King-harpist bold ;
He 's proud of his line, he 's erect as the pine
    That springs on the mountains old.
Through the hardy North, when his song goes forth,
    It rings like the clash of steel ;
Yet we have not a fear, for his heart 's sincere,
    And his blasts we love to feel.

            Then, hi ! for the storm,
            The wintry storm,
        That maketh the stars grow dim ;
            Not a nerve shall fail,
            Not a heart shall quail,
        When he rolls his grand old hymn.

Oh, hale and gay is that Norse King grey,
    And his limbs are both stout and strong ;
His eye is as keen as a falchion's sheen
    When it sweeps to avenge a wrong.
The Aurora's dance is his merry glance,
    As it speeds through the starry fields ;
And his anger falls upon Odin's halls
    Like the crash of a thousand shields.

            Then, hi ! for the storm, &c.
    34

CHARLES SANGSTER

His stately front has endured the brunt
  Of Scythian rack and gale,
As the vengeful years clashed their icy spears
  On the boss of his glancing mail ;
When he steps in his pride from his halls so wide,
  He laughs with a wild refrain ;
And the Elfins start from the iceberg's heart,
  And echo his laugh again.

      Then, hi ! for the storm, &c.

When the woods are stirred by the antlered herd,
  He comes like a Nimrod bold,
And the forest groans as his mighty tones
  Swoop down on the startled fold ;
In his mantle white he defies the Night,
  With the air of a King so free ;
Then hurrah for the rune, the North-King's rune,
  For his sons, his sons are we !

      Then, hi ! for the storm, &c.

24.   *The Rapid*

ALL peacefully gliding,
  The waters dividing,
The indolent batteau moved slowly along,
  The rowers, light-hearted,
  From sorrow long parted,
Beguiled the dull moments with laughter and song ;

CHARLES SANGSTER

' Hurrah for the rapid ! that merrily, merrily
   Gambols and leaps on its tortuous way ;
Soon we will enter it, cheerily, cheerily,
   Pleased with its freshness, and wet with its spray.'

   More swiftly careering,
   The wild rapid nearing,
They dash down the stream like a terrified steed ;
   The surges delight them,
   No terrors affright them,
Their voices keep pace with the quickening speed ;
' Hurrah for the rapid ! that merrily, merrily
   Shivers its arrows against us in play ;
Now we have entered it, cheerily, cheerily,
   Our spirits as light as its feathery spray.'

   Fast downward they're dashing,
   Each fearless eye flashing,
Though danger awaits them on every side ;
   Yon rock—see it frowning !
   They strike—they are drowning !
But downward they speed with the merciless tide ;
No voice cheers the rapid, that angrily, angrily
   Shivers their bark in its maddening play ;
Gaily they entered it—heedlessly, recklessly,
   Mingling their lives with its treacherous spray !

CHARLES SANGSTER

25.   *Hesperus*

A Legend of the Stars

PRELUDE

THE Stars are heaven's ministers;
  Right royally they teach
God's glory and omnipotence,
  In wondrous lowly speech.
All eloquent with music as
  The tremblings of a lyre,
To him that hath an ear to hear
  They speak in words of fire.

Not to learnèd sages only
  Their whisperings come down;
The monarch is not glorified
  Because he wears a crown.
The humblest soldier in the camp
  Can win the smile of Mars,
And 'tis the lowliest spirits hold
  Communion with the stars.

Thoughts too refined for utterance,
  Ethereal as the air,
Crowd through the brain's dim labyrinths,
  And leave their impress there;
As far along the gleaming void
  Man's tender glances roll,
Wonder usurps the throne of speech,
  But vivifies the soul.

Oh, heaven-cradled mysteries,
   What sacred paths ye've trod—
Bright, jewelled scintillations from
   The chariot-wheels of God !
When in the spirit He rode forth,
   With vast creative aim,
These were His footprints left behind,
   To magnify His name !

26.   *Song for Canada*

SONS of the race whose sires
   Aroused the martial flame
      That filled with smiles
      The triune Isles,
Through all their heights of fame !
With hearts as brave as theirs,
With hopes as strong and high,
      We'll ne'er disgrace
      The honoured race
Whose deeds can never die.
   Let but the rash intruder dare
      To touch our darling strand,
         The martial fires
         That thrilled our sires
      Would flame throughout the land.

Our lakes are deep and wide,
Our fields and forests broad ;
      With cheerful air
      We'll speed the share,

38

CHARLES SANGSTER

And break the fruitful sod ;
Till blest with rural peace,
Proud of our rustic toil,
    On hill and plain
    True kings we'll reign,
The victors of the soil.
  But let the rash intruder dare
    To touch our darling strand,
      The martial fires
      That thrilled our sires
    Would light him from the land.

Health smiles with rosy face
Amid our sunny dales,
    And torrents strong
    Fling hymn and song
Through all the mossy vales ;
Our sons are living men,
Our daughters fond and fair ;
    A thousand isles
    Where Plenty smiles,
Make glad the brow of Care.
  But let the rash intruder dare
    To touch our darling strand,
      The martial fires
      That thrilled our sires
    Would flame throughout the land.

And if in future years
One wretch should turn and fly,

Let weeping Fame
Blot out his name
From Freedom's hallowed sky ;
Or should our sons e'er prove
A coward, traitor race,—
Just Heaven ! frown
In thunder down
T' avenge the foul disgrace !
But let the rash intruder dare
To touch our darling strand,
The martial fires
That thrilled our sires
Would light him from the land.

27.   *The Red Men*

MY footsteps press where, centuries ago,   [won.
The Red Men fought and conquered ; lost and
Whole tribes and races, gone like last year's snow,
    Have found the Eternal Hunting-Grounds, and run
The fiery gauntlet of their active days,
    Till few are left to tell the mournful tale :
And these inspire us with such wild amaze
    They seem like spectres passing down a vale
Steeped in uncertain moonlight, on their way
Towards some bourne where darkness blinds the day,
    And night is wrapped in mystery profound.
We cannot lift the mantle of the past :
    We seem to wander over hallowed ground :
We scan the trail of Thought, but all is overcast.

40

CHARLES SANGSTER

28.   *The Little Shoes*

HER little shoes ! we sit and muse
    Upon the dainty feet that wore them ;
By day and night our souls' delight
    Is just to dream and ponder o'er them.
We hear them patter on the floor,
    In either hand a toy or rattle ;
And what speaks to our hearts the more—
    Her first sweet words of infant prattle.

I see the face so fair, and trace
    The dark-blue eye that flashed so clearly ;
The rose-bud lips, the finger-tips
    She learned to kiss—oh, far too dearly
The pearly hands turned up to mine,
    The tiny arms my neck caressing ;
Her smile, that made our life divine,
    Her silvery laugh—her kiss, a blessing.

Her winning ways, that made the days
    Elysian in their grace so tender,
Through which Love's child our souls beguiled
    For seeming ages starred with splendour :
No wonder that the angel-heirs
    Did win our darling life's-joy from us,
For she was theirs—not all our prayers
    Could keep her from the Land of Promise.

29.   *Viger Square*

HERE in this quiet garden shade,
    Whose blossoms spread their blooms before me,
The world's gay cheats,—life's masquerade,
Like evil ghosts from memory fade,
    And calm and holy thoughts come o'er me.

Ambrosial haunt ; the orient light
    Falls golden on thy soft seclusion ;
And like the lone and shadowy night,
Grim care, abashed, has taken flight,
    And joys gleam forth in rich profusion.

These odorous flowers that feast the bee,
    Those mimic fountains sunward leaping,
And yon red rowans on the tree,
That bring my childhood back to me,
    With hallowed scenes of Memory's keeping.

All these, and more, with beauty clad,
    Invite the city's weary mortals—
The pale-faced maid, the widow sad,
And sinking merchant, growing mad,
    To muse within these peaceful portals.

Here is the stone that sages sought,
    Here the famed lamp of blest Aladdin ;
Objects that tell ambitious thought,
' All that thy greed hath ever caught
    Cannot, like us, console and gladden.'

JOHN F. M'DONNELL

30.   *The Voyageur's Song*

WE track the herds o'er the prairies wide,
   Through the length of the summer day ;
And guide the canoe on the rapid's tide,
   Where the waters flash in the ray ;
Where the silvery scales of the salmon glance
   On the bosom of the pool ;
And we rest our wearied limbs at eve,
   In the shade of the pine-trees cool,
Let others toil for golden store ;
   For riches little we care ;
      Oh, the happiest life
      In this world of strife
   Is that of a Voyageur.

When the red sun sinks in the golden west,
   At evening when he goes
With ministering hosts of the golden clouds,
   To seek the night's repose—
We pitch our tents on the soft green sward,
   And we light our evening fire,
And we mingle strains of our Northern land
   With the notes of the forest choir.
Time flies along, with jest and song,
   For our merry men are there ;
      Oh, there 's not a life
      In this world of strife
   Like that of a Voyageur.

JOHN F. M'DONNELL

Oh, sweet and soft are our couches made
  With the broad green summer leaves,
And the curtains spread above the head
  Are those which Nature weaves.
The tall oak and the spreading elm
  Are twined in a tangled screen,—
Surpassing far all the magic skill
  Of the sculptor's art e'er seen.
We shun the noise of the busy world,
  For there 's crime and misery there ;
    And the happiest life
    In this world of strife
  Is that of a Voyageur.

J. R. RAMSAY

31.   *November. A Dirge*

DEPARTING wild birds gather
  On the high branches, ere they haste away,
Singing their farewell to the frigid ether
  And fading day,
To sport no more on withered mead or heather ;
  No longer gay.

The little cricket's singing
  Sounds lonely in the crisp and yellow leaves,
Like bygone tones of tenderness upbringing
  A thought that grieves :
A bell upon a ruined turret ringing
  On Sabbath eves.

44

J. R. RAMSAY

The ' tempest-loving raven ',
  Pilot of storms across the silent sky,
Soars loftily along the heaving heaven
  With doleful cry,
Uttering lone dirges.   Thistle-beards are driven
  Where the winds sigh.

And yet here is a flower
  Still lingering, by the changing season spared,
And a lone bird within a leafless bower—
  Two friends, who dared
To share the shadows of misfortune's hour,
  Though unprepared.

PAMELIA S. VINING-YULE

32.   *The Beechnut Gatherer*

ALL over the earth like a mantle,
  Golden, and green, and grey,
Crimson, and scarlet, and yellow,
  The Autumn foliage lay.
The sun of the Indian Summer
  Laughed at the bare old trees,
As they shook their leafless branches
  In the soft autumnal breeze.

I walked where the leaves the softest,
  The brightest, and goldenest lay ;
And I thought of a forest hill-side
  And an Indian Summer day,

45

PAMELIA S. VINING-YULE

An eager, little child-face,
  O'er the fallen leaves that bent,
As she gathered her cup of beechnuts
  With innocent content.

I thought of the small brown fingers,
  Gleaning them one by one;
With the partridge drumming near her
  In the forest bare and dun,
And the jet-black squirrel winking
  His saucy jealous eye
At those tiny, pilfering fingers,
  From his sly nook up on high.

Ah! barefooted little maiden,
  With thy bonnetless, sunburnt brow!
Thou glean'st no more on the hill-side---
  Where art thou gleaning now?
I knew by the lifted glances
  Of the dark, imperious eye,
That the tall trees bending o'er thee
  Would not shelter thee by and by.

The cottage by the brook-side,
  With its mossy roof, is gone;
The cattle have left the uplands,
  The young lambs left the lawn;
Gone are thy blue-eyed sister,
  And thy brother's laughing brow;—
And the beechnuts lie ungathered
  On the lonely hill-side now.

What have the returning seasons
   Brought to thy heart since then,
In thy long and weary wand'rings
   In the paths of busy men ?
Has the Angel of grief or of gladness
   Set his seal upon thy brow ?
Maiden ! joyous or tearful,
   Where art thou gleaning now ?

33.   *Patience*

I SAW how the patient Sun
   Hasted untiringly
The self-same old race to run ;
   Never aspiringly
Seeking some other road
   Through the blue heaven
Than the one path which God
   Long since had given ;—
   And I said, ' Patient Sun,
   Teach me my race to run,
   Even as thine is done,
     Steadfastly ever ;
   Weakly, impatiently
     Wandering never ! '

I saw how the patient Earth
   Sat uncomplainingly,
While in his boisterous mirth,
   Winter disdainingly

47

Mocked at her steadfast trust
  That from its icy chain
Spring her imprisoned dust
  Soon would release again ;—
  And I said, ' Patient Earth,
  Biding thy hour of dearth,
  Waiting the voice of mirth
    Soon to rewaken,
  Teach me like thee to trust,
    Steadfast, unshaken ! '

THOMAS D'ARCY M'GEE

34. *Jacques Cartier*

IN the seaport of Saint Malo 'twas a smiling morn
  in May,
When the Commodore Jacques Cartier to the westward sailed away ;
In the crowded old Cathedral all the town were on
  their knees
For the safe return of kinsmen from the undiscovered
  seas ;
And every autumn blast that swept o'er pinnacle and
  pier
Filled manly hearts with sorrow, and gentle hearts
  with fear.

A year passed o'er Saint Malo—again came round the day,
When the Commodore Jacques Cartier to the westward sailed away ;

48

But no tidings from the absent had come the way they
    went,
And tearful were the vigils that many a maiden spent ;
And manly hearts were filled with gloom, and gentle
    hearts with fear,
When no tidings came from Cartier at the closing of
    the year.

But the earth is as the Future, it hath its hidden side,
And the Captain of Saint Malo was rejoicing in his
    pride
In the forests of the North—while his townsmen
    mourned his loss,
He was rearing on Mount-Royal the fleur-de-lis and
    cross ;
And when two months were over and added to the
    year,
Saint Malo hailed him home again, cheer answering to
    cheer.

He told them of a region, hard, ironbound, and cold,
Where no seas of pearl abounded, nor mines of shining
    gold,
Where the wind from Thulê freezes the word upon
    the lip,
And the ice in spring comes sailing athwart the early
    ship ;
He told them of the frozen scene until they thrill'd
    with fear,
And piled fresh fuel on the hearth to make them better
    cheer.

THOMAS D'ARCY M'GEE

But when he changed the strain—he told how soon
    are cast
In early Spring the fetters that hold the waters fast ;
How the Winter causeway broken is drifted out to sea,
And rills and rivers sing with pride the anthem of the
    free ;
How the magic wand of Summer clad the landscape
    to his eyes,
Like the dry bones of the just when they wake in
    Paradise.

He told them of the Algonquin braves—the hunters
    of the wild ;
Of how the Indian mother in the forest rocks her child ;
Of how, poor souls, they fancy in every living thing
A spirit good or evil, that claims their worshipping ;
Of how they brought their sick and maim'd for him
    to breathe upon,
And of the wonders wrought for them through the
    Gospel of St. John.

He told them of the river, whose mighty current gave
Its freshness for a hundred leagues to ocean's briny
    wave ;
He told them of the glorious scene presented to his
    sight,
What time he reared the cross and crown on Hoche-
    laga's height,
And of the fortress cliff that keeps of Canada the key,
And they welcomed back Jacques Cartier from his
    perils o'er the sea.

50

THOMAS D'ARCY M'GEE

35.   *The Arctic Indian's Faith*

WE worship the Spirit that walks unseen
    Through our land of ice and snow ;
We know not His face, we know not His place,
    But His presence and power we know.

Does the buffalo need the pale-face's word
    To find his pathway far ?
What guide has he to the hidden ford,
    Or where the green pastures are ?

Who teacheth the moose that the hunter's gun
    Is peering out of the shade ?
Who teacheth the doe and the fawn to run
    In the track the moose has made ?

Him do we follow, Him do we fear—
    Spirit of earth and sky ;
Who hears with the Wapiti's eager ear
    His poor red children's cry.

Whose whisper we note in every breeze
    That stirs the birch canoe ;
Who hangs the reindeer moss on the trees
    For the food of the caribou.

That Spirit we worship who walks, unseen,
    Through our land of ice and snow ;
We know not His face, we know not His place,
    But His presence and power we know.

MRS. R. A. FAULKNER

36.　　　*Frost on the Window*

O'ER the window crept the hoary frost,
　With many a wayward freak and curious antic,
In varied lines, that quaintly blent and crossed
　　In tracery romantic.

Here, bloomed a wreath of pure pale ghostly flowers,
　As hueless as the faded cheek of death ;
There, rose tall pinnacles and Gothic towers,
　　That melted with a breath ;

With trees and foliage rich—the tinted oak,
　The willow, wan and still, like settled grief,
The hazel, easy bent, but hardly broke,
　　And varying maple leaf.

The gentle moonbeam kissed the silvery pane
　With a most sister-like and chaste caress,
As if it fain a fellowship would claim
　　With such pure loveliness.

And still more beautiful the magic ray
　Made all it rested on, leaf, flower, and tree ;
And lingered there, like innocence at play
　　With stainless purity.

52

GEORGE MURRAY

37. *To a Humming-Bird in a Garden*

BLITHE playmate of the Summer time,
  Admiringly I greet thee ;
Born in old England's misty clime,
  I scarcely hoped to meet thee.

Com'st thou from forest of Peru,
  Or from Brazil's savannahs,
Where flowers of every dazzling hue
  Flaunt, gorgeous as Sultanas ?

Thou scannest me with doubtful gaze,
  Suspicious little stranger !
Fear not, thy burnished wings may blaze
  Secure from harm or danger.

Now here, now there, thy flash is seen,
  Like some stray sunbeam darting,
With scarce a second's space between
  Its coming and departing.

Mate of the bird that lives sublime
  In Pat's immortal blunder,
Spied in two places at a time,
  Thou challengest our wonder.

53

GEORGE MURRAY

Suspended by thy slender bill,
   Sweet blooms thou lov'st to rifle ;
The subtle perfumes they distil
   Might well thy being stifle.

Surely the honey-dew of flowers
   Is slightly alcoholic,
Or why, through burning August hours,
   Dost thou pursue thy frolic ?

What though thy throatlet never rings
   With music, soft or stirring ;
Still, like a spinning-wheel, thy wings
   Incessantly are whirring.

How dearly I would love to see
   Thy tiny cara sposa,
As full of sensibility
   As any coy mimosa !

They say, when hunters track her nest,
   Where two warm pearls are lying,
She boldly fights, though sore distrest,
   And sends the brigands flying.

What dainty epithets thy tribes
   Have won from men of science !
Pedantic and poetic scribes
   For once are in alliance.

Crested Coquette, and Azure Crown,
   Sun Jewel, Ruby-Throated,
With Flaming Topaz, Crimson Down,
   Are names that may be quoted.

54

GEORGE MURRAY

Such titles aim to paint the hues
　　That on the darlings glitter,
And were we for a week to muse,
　　We scarce could light on fitter

Farewell, bright bird ! I envy thee,
　　Gay rainbow-tinted rover ;
Would that my life, like thine, were free
　　From care till all is over !

JOHN HUNTER-DUVAR

38   ## *Twilight Song*

THE mountain peaks put on their hoods
　　　　Good night !
And the long shadows of the woods
　　Would fain the landscape cover quite.
The timid pigeons homeward fly,
Scared by the whoop-owl's eerie cry,
　　　　Whoo-oop ! whoo-oop !
As like a fiend he flitteth by ;
　　The ox to stall, the fowl to coop,
The old man to his nightcap warm,
　　Young men and maids to slumbers light.
Sweet Mary, keep our souls from harm !
　　　　Good night ! good night !

55

39. *Mermaid's Song*

A GALLANT fleet sailed out to sea
  With the pennons streaming merrily ;
On the hulls the tempest lit,
And the great ships split
    In the gale,
And the foaming fierce sea-horses
Hurled the fragments in their forces
To the ocean deeps,
Where the kraken sleeps,
    And the whale.

The men are in the ledges' clefts,
Dead, but with motion of living guise
Their bodies are rocking there,
Monstrous sea-fish and efts
Stare at them with glassy eyes
As their limbs are stirred, and their hair.

Moan, O sea !
O death at once and the grave,
And sorrow in passing, O cruel wave !
Let the resonant sea-caves ring,
And the sorrowful surges sing,
For the dead men rest but restlessly.

We do keep account of them,
And sing an ocean requiem
    For the brave.

SARAH ANNE CURZON

40.   *The Loyalists*

YE, who with your blood and sweat
    Watered the furrows of this land,—
See where upon a nation's brow,
    In honour's front, ye proudly stand !

Who for her pride abased your own,
    And gladly on her altar laid
All bounty of the older world,
    All memories that your glory made,

And to her service bowed your strength,
    Took labour for your shield and crest ;
See where upon a nation's brow,
    Her diadem, ye proudly rest !

CHARLES PELHAM MULVANEY

41.   *Poppaea at the Theatre*

DARK tresses made rich with all treasures,
    Earth's gold-dust, and pearls of the sea,—
She is splendid as Rome that was Caesar's,
    And cruel as Rome that was free !

Could I paint her but once as I found her,
    From her porphyry couch let her lean,
With the reek of the circus around her—
    Who is centre and soul of the scene ;

57

CHARLES PELHAM MULVANEY

Grey eyes that glance keen as the eagle
  When he swoops to his prey from on high ;
Bold arms by the red gold made regal—
  White breast never vexed with a sigh ;

And haughty her mien as of any
  Her sires whom the foemen knew well,
As they rode through the grey mist at Cannae,
  Ere consul with consular fell.

Unabashed in her beauty of figure—
  Heavy limbs and thick tresses uncurled
To our gaze, give the grace and the vigour
  Of the race that has conquered the world.

And fierce with the blood of the heroes—
  In their sins and their virtues sublime—
Sits the Queen of the world that is Nero's,
  And as keen for a kiss or a crime !

But the game that amuses her leisure
  Loses zest as the weaker gives way ;
And the victor looks up for her pleasure—
  Shall he spare with the sword-point or slay ?

Half-grieving she gathers her tresses,
  Now the hour for the game has gone by ;
And those soft arms, so sweet for caresses,
  Point prone as she signs, ' Let him die.'

THEODORE HARDING RAND

42. *The Water-Lily*

PURE lily, open on the breast
  Of toiling waters' much unrest,
   Thy simple soul mounts up in worship
Like ecstasy of a spirit blest !

Thy wealth of ivory and gold,
All that thou hast, thou dost unfold !
   Fixed in the unseen thy life breathes upward
A heavenly essence from out earth's mould.

Now comes the chill and dusk of night,—
Folds up thy precious gold and white !
   Thy casket sinks within veiled bosom,.
To ope the richer in morrow's light.

43. *The Whitethroat*

SHY bird of the silver arrows of song,
  That cleave our Northern air so clear,
Thy notes prolong, prolong,
   I listen, I hear :
' I—love—dear—Canada,
            Canada, Canada.'

O plumes of the pointed dusky fir,
   Screen of a swelling patriot heart,
The copse is all astir,
   And echoes thy part ! . . .

59

Now willowy reeds tune their silver flutes
    As the noise of the day dies down ;
And silence strings her lutes,
    The Whitethroat to crown. . . .

O bird of the silver arrows of song,
    Shy poet of Canada dear,
Thy notes prolong, prolong,
    We listen, we hear :
' I—love—dear—Canada,
                Canada, Canada.'

W. KIRBY

44.   *Thunderstorm in August*

BUT when fierce August suns, careering high,
    Gaze hot and silent from the brazen sky ;
When bird and beast forsake the open glade,
And pant all mute within the sultry shade ;
When not a breath doth stir the lightest leaf,
And springs and brooks dried up deny relief ;
While Nature lies exhausted in the throes
Of parching thirst, the sharpest of her woes ;
Then, lo ! a small dark cloud, all fringed with red,
Above th' horizon lifts its liquid head ;
Surveys the scene, and larger grows to view,
While all the legions of the storm pursue.

W. KIRBY

The muttering thunder with unceasing din
Proclaims the strife of elements within ;
And lurid flashes flood the murky clouds,
As faster on they follow, crowds on crowds.

Eclipsed the sun, his fires at once allayed,
Falls o'er the quaking earth a dreadful shade ;
A thousand birds aloft in terror rise
And seek the safest haunts, with piercing cries ;
The leaves, they tremble in the breathless woods,
And sighing trees confess th' approaching floods.
At once, 'mid clouds of dust and flying leaves,
The whirlwind sweeps aloft the scattered sheaves ;
Sharp lightning rends the black and marble skies,
And thousand-voiced the pealing thunder flies.
The shattered boughs upon the tempest ride,
And rocking forests groan from side to side ;
While cataracts of rain in deluge pour,
And sweep the smoking land with ceaseless roar.

The wild tornado passes, and the sun
With golden rays peeps through the clouds of dun.
Green Nature glistens, and the piping bird
Within the dripping grove is fluttering heard ;
While down the streaming gullies, furrowed wide,
The rushing waters pour on every side,
And earth refreshed emerges from the storm
With smiling face and renovated form.

JOHN READE

45. *Hastings*

I

OCTOBER'S woods are bright and gay, a thousand
colours vie
To win the golden smiles the Sun sends gleaming
through the sky ;
And though the flowers are dead and gone, one garden
seems the earth,
For in God's world, as one charm dies, another starts
to birth.

II

To every season is its own peculiar beauty given,
In every age of mortal men we see the Hand of Heaven ;
And century to century utters a glorious speech,
And peace to war, and war to peace, eternal lessons
teach.

III

O grand old woods, your forest-sires were thus as
bright and gay,
Before the axe's murderous voice had spoiled their
sylvan play ;
When other axes smote our sires, and laid them stiff
and low
On Hastings' unforgotten field, eight hundred years
ago.

JOHN READE

IV

Eight hundred years ago, long years, before Jacques
    Cartier clomb
The Royal Height, where now no more the red men
    fearless roam !
Eight hundred years ago, long years before Columbus
    came
From stately Spain to find the world that ought to
    bear his name !

V

The Sussex woods were bright and red on that October
    morn,
And Sussex soil was red with blood before the next
    was born ;
But from that red united clay another race did start
On the great stage of destiny to act a noble part.

VI

So God doth mould, as pleaseth Him, the nations of
    His choice ;
Now, in the battle-cry is heard His purifying voice ;
And now, with Orphic strains of peace he draws to
    nationhood
The scattered tribes that dwell apart by mountain,
    sea, and wood.

VII

He took the lonely poet Celt and taught him Roman
    lore ;
Then from the wealds of Saxony He brought the sons
    of Thor ;

Next from his craggy home the Dane came riding o'er
    the sea ;
And last, came William with his bands of Norman
    chivalry.

VIII

And now, as our young nationhood is struggling into
    birth,
God grant its infant pulse may beat with our fore-
    fathers' worth !
And, as we gather into one, let us recall with pride
That we are of the blood of those who fought when
    Harold died.

46.   *In my Heart*

IN my heart are many chambers through which I
    wander free ;
  Some are furnished, some are empty, some are
    sombre, some are light ;
Some are open to all comers, of some I keep the key ;
  And I enter in the stillness of the night.

But there 's one I never enter—it is closed to even me !
  Only once its door was opened, and it shut for ever-
    more ;
And though sounds of many voices gather round it
    like a sea,
  It is silent, ever silent, as the shore.

JOHN READE

In that chamber, long ago, my love's casket was con-
    cealed,
    And the jewel that it sheltered I knew only one
      could win ;
And my soul foreboded sorrow, should that jewel be
    revealed,
    And I almost hopèd that none might enter in.

Yet day and night I lingered by that fatal chamber
    door,
    Till she came at last, my darling one, of all the earth
      my own ;
And she entered—then she vanished with my jewel
    which she wore ;
    And the door was closed—and I was left alone.

She gave me back no jewel, but the spirit of her eyes
    Shone with tenderness a moment, as she closed that
      chamber door,
And the memory of that moment is all I have to
    prize—
    But that, at least, is mine for evermore.

Was she conscious, when she took it, that the jewel
    was my love ?
    Did she think it but a bauble she might wear or
      toss aside ?
I know not, I accuse not, but I hope that it may prove
    A blessing, though she spurn it in her pride.

JOHN READE

47. *In Memoriam of October 25, 1854*

(Written on the occasion of the Balaclava Festival.)

OH ! say not that the chivalry
   That our brave fathers led
To noble deeds of bravery, ·
   In us their sons is dead !
For the same blood that leaped of yore
   Upon the battle-plains
Of Crécy and of Agincourt,
   Still leaps within our veins.

The times are changed; the arts of peace
   Are cherished more than then,
But, until wars for ever cease,
   Our country shall have men
To draw the sword for country's good,
   To battle for the right,
To shed their heart's best drop of blood
   In many a hard-fought fight.

All honour to the good and brave
   Who fought in days of old,
And shame upon the sordid knave
   Whose heart's so dull and cold
As not to feel an honest glow
   Of patriotic pride,
When he is told that long ago
   Such heroes lived and died.

JOHN READE

Then let us to their memory give
　A grateful, manly thought,
And, if we prize them, let us live
　As nobly as they fought ;
Each life is but a battle-field,
　The Wrong against the Right.
Then think, when Right to Wrong would yield,
　Of Balaclava's fight.

JOHN T. LESPERANCE
48.　　　　*Empire First*

SHALL we break the plight of youth,
　And pledge us to an alien love ?
No !　We hold our faith and truth
　Trusting to the God above.
Stand, Canadians, firmly stand
Round the flag of fatherland !

Britain bore us in her flank,
　Britain nursed us at our birth,
Britain reared us to our rank
　'Mid the nations of the earth.
Stand, Canadians, firmly stand
Round the flag of fatherland !

In the hour of pain and dread,
　In the gathering of the storm,
Britain raised above our head
　Her broad shield and sheltering arm.
Stand, Canadians, firmly stand
Round the flag of fatherland !

JOHN T. LESPERANCE

O triune Kingdom of the brave,
  O sea-girt Island of the free,
O Empire of the land and wave,
  Our hearts, our hands, are all for thee !
Stand, Canadians, firmly stand
Round the flag of fatherland !

JOHN J. PROCTER

49.   *Light*

BREAK o'er the sea ! Break on the night !
  Ever blessèd and holy light ;
Shed but one ray, but one joyous beam,
Wherever the eastern waters gleam—
But one small ray, for the night is dark,
And the ocean waits for the first bright spark ;
Others are longing too for thee :
    Break o'er the sea ! Break o'er the sea !

O dawn ! O rosy-fingered dawn !
Come up and herald another morn ;
Come, till the dark mists fly away ;
Come, till the night gives place to day ;
Come, where the deep black waters boom ;
Come, through the veil of the sullen gloom ;
All things are longing, O light, for thee :
    Break o'er the sea ! Break o'er the sea !

63

JOHN J. PROCTER

O day ! O happy, happy day !
Chase the gloomy shadows away.
Though Nature's slumbers seem calm and deep,
There are those on earth who cannot sleep—
Those who in toil alone are blest—
Those who in labour alone find rest.
Hearts that are breaking have need of thee :
    Break o'er the sea ! Break o'er the sea !

O light ! O tender, tender light !
There came a cry through the livelong night ;
Wherever a mortal foot has trod,
A cry of woe to a loving God,
From those who would drink of the fabled wave
That gives forgetfulness long as the grave :
Sorrowing souls have need of thee :
    Break o'er the sea ! Break o'er the sea !

O waves that were moaning all night long,
Break out, and join in the angels' song ;
Thunder it out with shock on shock
Into the ears of the dull hard rock :
Whisper it low to the far-off strand
Where the riplets lazily laugh on the sand,
Till earth shall echo from flower to tree,
    Break o'er the sea ! Break o'er the sea !

O type of the Everlasting Day !
Come from the East land far away—
The land whence once came a holy voice
Bidding all mourning hearts rejoice ;

Come, and recall its echoes now,
Flash on the darkened and sullen brow,
Bid all doubts and all sorrows flee :
    Break o'er the sea ! Break o'er the sea !

O Sun, rise up from thy watery bed !
Rise, till the shades of night have fled !
Sweep on, on thy mission, and linger not,
With rays of love, on each sacred spot,
Where he, the Pure One, for sinners bled,
Where earth once covered her Maker's head—
He that made thee is calling to thee,
    Break o'er the sea ! Break o'er the sea !

50.   *Dead*

OH, let me dream for a while
    Under the winter sky;
Dream of the light of a vanished smile,
    And the hopes of a day gone by;
Dream of a lovely face,
    And the grace of a lovely head,
And the form that I clasped in a fond embrace—
    Let me dream for a while of the dead.

Dead ! can it be I am here
    Whispering this to my heart ?
Dead ! and I have not one welcome tear
    To soften the inward smart !

JOHN J. PROCTER

Dead ! and I cannot pray,
  For I think of my love that is gone,
And the hope that was withered in one short day
  Has blasted my heart to stone.

What have I left but to dream
  Of my love that is laid in her rest,
To live as I live, for my life's years seem
  But an empty dream at the best !
Everything round is still
  And white as a new-made shroud,
From the snow-clad lea to the pines on the hill,
  And the fleecy veil of the cloud.

Here on the snow I lie
  Seeking a balm for care,
Looking up to the blank of the sky,
  And the blue of the fathomless air.
Hark ! how the chill winds wail,
  And shiver and moan in their flight ;
What a depth of woe in the sorrowful tale
  They tell in the ear of the night !

What is it that makes them sad ?
  Do they miss the grace of the flowers,
And sigh for the time when their breath was glad
  With the sweets of the summer hours ?
Ye do well, chill winds, to rave,
  For the day of your brides has fled,
The earth lies heavy and cold on their grave,
  They are dead—and she too is dead !

NICHOLAS FLOOD DAVIN

51.   *Illusion*

(From *Eos, an Epic of the Dawn*)

ILLUSION makes the better part of life.
  Happy self-conjurers, deceived, we win
Delight, and, ruled by fancy, live in dreams ;—
The mood, the hour, the standpoint, rules the scene ;
The past, the present, the to-be, weave charms ;
White-flashing memory's fleet footsteps fly,
And all the borders of her way are pied
With flowers full glad e'en when their roots touch
    quick
With pain.　With tears upon his dimpled cheek
Forth steps the infant Joy and, laughing, mocks
At care.　In time smiles play upon the cheek
Of pale Regret, who grows transformed, and stands
A pensive queen, more fair than boisterous Mirth.
The present's odorous with leaves of trees
Long dead, and dead defacing woods and thorns,
And past the cloud that glowered, the blast that smote,
And out from never-to-be-trodden days
Hope smiles, and airs from dawns we're never doomed
To see, come rich with fragrance, fresh with power,
Profuse of promises of golden days,
And join the necromancy of the past,
Mingling the magic which makes up our lives.

JOHN CAMPBELL, DUKE OF ARGYLL

52.   *Canada*

A National Hymn

FROM our Dominion never
   Take Thy protecting hand !
United, Lord, for ever
   Keep Thou our fathers' land !
From where Atlantic terrors
   Our hardy seamen train,
To where the salt sea mirrors
   The vast Pacific chain.
Ay one with her whose thunder
   Keeps world-watch with the hours,
Guard Freedom's home and wonder,
   This Canada of ours.

Fair days of fortune send her,
   Be Thou her Shield and Sun !
Our land, our flag's Defender,
   Unite our hearts as one !
One flag, one land, upon her
   May every blessing rest !
For loyal faith and honour
   Her children's deeds attest.
Ay one with her, &c.

No stranger's foot, insulting,
   Shall tread our country's soil ;
While stand her sons exulting
   For her to live and toil.

73

JOHN CAMPBELL, DUKE OF ARGYLL

She hath the victor's guerdon,
   Hers are the conquering hours,
No foeman's yoke shall burden
   This Canada of ours.
Ay one with her, &c.

Our sires, when times were sorest,
   Asked none but aid Divine,
And cleared the tangled forest,
   And wrought the buried mine.
They tracked the floods and fountains,
   And won, with master-hand,
Far more than gold in mountains,
   The glorious Prairie-land.
Ay one with her, &c.

O Giver of earth's treasure,
   Make Thou our nation strong;
Pour forth Thine hot displeasure
   On all who work her wrong!
To our remotest border
   Let plenty still increase,
Let Liberty and Order
   Bid ancient feuds to cease.
Ay one with her, &c.

May Canada's fair daughters
   Keep house for hearts as bold
As theirs who o'er the waters
   Came hither first of old.

JOHN CAMPBELL, DUKE OF ARGYLL

The pioneers of nations !
  They showed the world the way ;
'Tis ours to keep their stations,
  And lead the van to-day.
Ay one with her, &c.

Inheritors of glory,
  O countrymen ! we swear
To guard the flag whose story
  Shall onward victory bear.
Where'er through earth's far regions
  Its triple crosses fly,
For God, for home, our legions
  Shall win, or fighting die !
Ay one with her, &c.

53.   *Quebec*

O FORTRESS city, bathed by streams,
  Majestic as thy memories great,
Where mountain-floods and forests mate
The grandeur of the glorious dreams,
  Born of the hero-hearts who died
  In founding here an empire's pride.

Who hath not known delight, whose feet
  Hath paced thy streets, thy terrace way ;
  From rampart sod or bastion grey
Hath marked thy sea-like river greet

75

JOHN CAMPBELL, DUKE OF ARGYLL

The bright and peopled banks which shine
    In front of the far mountain's line ;
Thy glittering roofs below, the play
    Of currents where the ships entwine
Their spars, or laden pass away.

As we who joyously once rode
    Past guarded gates to trumpet sound,
    Along the devious ways that wound
O'er drawbridges, through moats, and showed
    The vast St. Lawrence flowing, belt
    The Orleans Isle, and seaward melt ;
Then by old walls with cannon crowned,
    Down stair-like streets, to where we felt
The soft winds blown o'er meadow ground.

Where flows the Charles past wharf and dock,
    And Learning from Laval looks down,
    And quiet convents grace the town ;
· There, swift to meet the battle-shock,
    Montcalm rushed on ; and eddying back
    Red slaughter marked the bridge's track ;
See now the shores with lumber brown,
    And girt with happy lands which lack
No loveliness of summer's crown.

Quiet hamlet alleys, border-filled
    With purple lilacs, poplars tall,
    Where flits the yellow-bird, and fall
The deep eave-shadows. There, when tilled

JOHN CAMPBELL, DUKE OF ARGYLL

The peasant's field or garden bed,
He rests content if o'er his head,
From silver spires, the church bells call
To gorgeous shrines, and prayers that gild
The simple hopes and lives of all.

54.   *Qu'Appelle Valley*

MORNING, lighting all the prairies,
Once of old came, bright as now,
To the twin cliffs, sloping wooded
From the vast plain's even brow:
When the sunken valley's levels
With the winding willowed stream,
Cried, ' Depart, night's mists and shadows;
Open-flowered, we love to dream ! '

Then in his canoe a stranger
Passing onward heard a cry;
Thought it called his name and answered,
But the voice would not reply;
Waited listening, while the glory
Rose to search each steep ravine,
Till the shadowed terraced ridges
Like the level vale were green.

Strange as when on Space the voices
Of the stars' hosannahs fell,
To this wilderness of beauty
Seemed his call ' Qu'Appelle ? Qu'Appelle ? '

For a day he tarried, hearkening,
  Wondering, as he went his way,
Whose the voice that gladly called him
  With the merry tones of day.

Was it God, who gave dumb Nature
  Voice and words to shout to one
Who, a pioneer, came, sunlike,
  Down the pathways of the sun ?
Harbinger of thronging thousands,
  Bringing plain, and vale, and wood,
Things the best and last created,
  Human hearts and brotherhood !

55.   *Alberta*

IN token of the love which thou hast shown
  For this wide land of freedom, I have named
  A province vast, and for its beauty famed,
By thy dear name to be hereafter known.
Alberta shall it be ! Her fountains thrown
  From alps unto three oceans, to all men
  Shall vaunt her loveliness e'en now ; and when,
Each little hamlet to a city grown,
And numberless as blades of prairie grass,
  Or the thick leaves in distant forest bower,
Great peoples hear the giant currents pass,
  Still shall the waters, bringing wealth and power,
Speak the loved name—land of silver springs—
Worthy the daughter of our English kings.

78

GRANT ALLEN

56.   *A Prayer*

A CROWNED caprice is god of this world ;
   On his stony breast are his white wings furled.
No ear to listen, no eye to see,
No heart to feel for a man hath he.
But his pitiless arm is swift to smite ;
And his mute lips utter one word of might,
'Mid the clash of gentler souls and rougher,
' Wrong must thou do, or wrong must suffer.'
Then grant, O dumb, blind god, at least that we
Rather the sufferers than the doers be.

JOHN E. LOGAN

57.   *The Squaw's Lament*

A BLOOD-RED ring hung round the moon,
   A blood-red ring, ah me ! ah me !
I heard the piping of the loon,
   A wounded loon, ah me !
And yet the eagle feathers rare
I trembling wove in my brave's hair.

He left me in the early morn,
   The early morn, ah me ! ah me !
The feathers swayed like stately corn—
   So like the corn, ah me !
A fierce wind swept across the plain,
The stately corn was snapt in twain.

JOHN E. LOGAN

They crushed in blood the hated race,
  The hated race, ah me ! ah me !
I only clasped a cold, blind face—
  His cold, dead face, ah me !
The blood-red ring hangs in my sight,
I hear the loon cry every night.

AGNES MAULE MACHAR

58.   *Untrodden Ways*

WHERE close the curving mountains drew,
  To clasp the stream in their embrace,
With every outline, shade and hue
  Reflected in its placid face,

The ploughman stops his team to watch
  The train, as swift it thunders by ;
Some distant glimpse of life to catch,
  He strains his eager, wistful eye.

His waiting horses patient stand
  With wonder in their gentle eyes,
As through the tranquil mountain land
  The snorting engine onward flies.

The morning freshness is on him,
  Just wakened from his balmy dreams ;
The wayfarers, all soiled and dim,
  Think longingly of mountain streams.
80

AGNES MAULE MACHAR

Oh, for the joyous mountain air,
　The long, delightful autumn day
Among the hills !—the ploughman there
　Must have perpetual holiday !

And he, as all day long he guides
　His steady plough with patient hand,
Thinks of the train that onward glides
　Into some new enchanted land,

Where, day by day, no plodding round
　Wearies the frame and dulls the mind,
Where life thrills keen to sight and sound,
　With ploughs and furrows left behind !

Even so to each the untrod ways
　Of life are touched by Fancy's glow,
That ever sheds its brightest rays
　Upon the paths we do not know !

59.　　*The Coming of the Spring*

WITH subtle presence the air is filling,
　Our pulses thrilling ;
What strange mysterious sense of gladness
　Transfused with sadness ;
Trembling in opal and purple hues
　That wake and melt in azure high,
Brooding in sunbeams that suffuse
　With the light of hope, the fields that lie
　Quiet and grey 'neath the sunset sky !

AGNES MAULE MACHAR

Thor's thunder-hammer hath waked the earth
   To a glad new birth—
The birth of the fresh, young, joyous spring,
   New blossoming—
Bidding the south wind softly blow,
   Loosing the tongues of the murmuring streams,
Sending the sap with a swifter flow
   Through the bare brown trees, and waking dreams
   Of summer shadows and golden gleams !

Down in the budding woods unseen,
   Amid mosses green,
The fair hepatica wakes to meet
   The hastening feet
Of the children that soon, with laughter sweet,
   Shall shout with glee to find it there,
And bear it homeward—the herald meet
   Of the countless bells and blossoms fair
   That shall ring sweet chimes on the balmy air.

And tiny ferns their fronds unbind
   By streams that wind—
Singing a song in soft undertones—
   O'er the smooth brown stones ;
And pure white lilies and purple phlox
   And violets yellow and white and grey,
And columbines gleaming from lichened rocks,
   And dogwood blossoms and snowy may,
   Shall wreathe with beauty each woodland way.

AGNES MAULE MACHAR

Soon, in the shadow of dewy leaves
   About our eaves,
The chorister-birds shall their matins ring,
   Sweet carolling ;
While, through the bowery orchard trees,
   All sprinkled with drifts of scented snow,
Comes the fragrant breath of the morning breeze,
   And over the long lush grass below
   Soft wavering shadows glide to and fro.

But when shall the better Spring arise
   Beneath purer skies—
The Spring that can never pass away
   Nor know decay—
Sending new joy through the stricken heart,
   Waking new life from the silent tomb,
Joining the souls that have moved apart,
Bidding earth's winter for ever depart,
   With incompleteness, pain, and gloom,
   Till—ransomed at last from its inwrought doom—
   It shall blossom forth in immortal bloom ?

AGNES MAULE MACHAR

60.   *Prayer for Dominion Day*

WITH head uplifted towards the Polar star,
   And feet half buried in the vines and corn,
Our country, of the nations latest born,
Stretches one hand the Atlantic's waves to bar,
The other—to the setting sun afar—
   Rolls back the wide Pacific towards the morn !
   And yet, methinks, distracted and forlorn
She looks—from things that were to things that are—
With doubtful eyes, that all uncertain sweep
   The wide horizon, as if searching there
For one strong love to make her pulses leap
   With one strong impulse ! Wayward passions tear
The heart that should be set in purpose deep,
   And cloud the eyes that should be raised in prayer !

O God of nations, who hast set her place
   Between the rising and the setting day,
   Her part in this world's changeful course to play,
Soothe the conflicting passions that we trace
In her unrestful eyes—grant her the grace
   To know the one true perfect love that may
   Give noble impulse to her onward way—
God's love, that doth all other loves embrace !
Gird her with panoply of truth and right
   In which she may go forth her fate to meet—
Ithuriel's spear, to crush with angel might
   The brood of darkness crouching at her feet ;
With faith to nerve her will and clear her sight,
   Till she shall round a destiny complete !

CHARLES MAIR

61.   *The Morning-Land*

THE light rains grandly from the distant wood,
   For in the wood the hermit sun is hid ;
So night draws back her curtains ebon-hued,
   To close them round some eastern pyramid.

The listless dew lies shining on the grass,
   And o'er the streams the light darts quick away,
And through the fields the morning sunbeams pass,
   Shot from the opening portals of the day.

Still upward mounts the tireless eremite,
   While all the herald birds make loud acclaim,
Till o'er the woods he rounds upon our sight,
   And lo ! the western world is all aflame.

From out the landscape lying 'neath the sun
   The last sea-smelling, cloud-like mists arise ;
The smoky woods grow clear, and, one by one,
   The meadow blossoms ope their winking eyes.

Now pleasèd Fancy starts with eager mien
   A-tiptoe, looking o'er the silent fields,
Where all the land is fresh and calm and green,
   And every flow'r its balmy incense yields.

And I, who am upon no business bent,
   A simple stroller through these dewy ways,
Feel that all things are with my future blent,
   Yet see them in the light of bygone days.

CHARLES MAIR

62.   *Innocence*

OFT have I met her
      In openings of the woods and pleasant ways,
   Where leaves beset her,
And hanging branches crowned her head with bays.

   Oft have I seen her walk
Through flower-deck'd fields unto the oaken pass
   Where knelt the chewing flock,
And lambkins gambolled round her on the grass.

   Oft have I seen her stand
By wandering brooks o'er which the willows met,
   Or where the meadow-land
Balmed the soft air with dew-mist drapery wet.

   Much patting of the wind
Had bloomed her cheek with colour of the rose ;
   Rare beauty was entwined
With locks and looks in movement or repose.

   Beneath her sloping neck
Her bosom-gourds swelled chastely, white as spray,
   Wind-tost—without a fleck—
The air which heaved them was less pure than they.

   Strolling in Evening's eye
There came unto her airy laughter-chimes,
   Nature's night-hymn and cry,
The music of the leaves and river rhymes.

86

CHARLES MAIR

The floriage of Spring
And Summer's coronals were hers in trust,
    Till came the Winter-King
To droop their sweetness into native dust.

    His sharp, embracing wind,
And wavering snow, or heaped in rimy hills,
    She loved ; aye ! she could bind
On Fancy's brow his charmèd icicles.

    The dingle and the glade,
The rock-ribbed wilderness, the talking trees
    Seemed fairer while she stayed,
And drank of their dim meanings and old ease.

    For Nature craved her, nursed
Her spirit at her mighty breast as one
    Who felt the forests' thirst,
The hunger of the mountains for the sun.

    Thoughts such as day unfolds
From starry quietude and noiseless sleep ;
    Scenes which the Fancy holds
In easy thraldom in her joyous keep.

    Visions of Duty's height,
And pious legends told at dimmest eve,
    Came thronging, faintly bright,
The habit of her inner life to weave.

CHARLES MAIR

Thus chiefly did she love
To soothe the hidden ruth, the bridled tear ;
   With counsel from above,
Alleviating woe, allaying fear.

   For all alive to pain,
Another's was her own ; Life's ceaseless care,
   Which loads with chain on chain
The heavenward spirit, she was wont to share.

   All this, and more, was hers—
What the sad soul remits to God alone ;
   What the fond heart avers
In secret helplessness before His throne.

   For He who made the light,
Earth and the biding stars, was all her guide.
   She worshipped in his sight,
She joyed, she wept, she flung away her pride.

   She thought of One who bore
The awful burden of the world's despair ;
   What could she give him more
Than helpful deeds, a simple life and fair ?

   She was, and is, for still
She lives and moves upon the grass-green earth,
   And, as of old, doth fill
Her heart with love, still mingling tears with mirth.

88

So wherefore cast about
For sect or creed from which no rancour spreads,
    Since we can make her out
By following the peaceful path she treads ?

    Though Truth is hard to find,
And blind belief is oft in error's th all ;
    Though unbelief is blind,
Though we who know a portion know not all——

    Yet she is self-revealed
Throughout the puzzled world we wander in,
    And free—though unrepealed
Her statutes—since she hath the power to sin.

    For what should not be makes
Her life sublime by putting it to test ;
    And in this wise awakes
The evil that is in us for the best.

63. *Stanzas from 'To a Morning Cloud'*

O GOLDEN shape ! Fair, full-blown flow'r of
    heaven !
Gift of the dawn and far-possessing sea !
Thou foster-child of sunshine and the free
Wild air of summer, wherefore art thou given
To mock us with delights which quickly flee
Th' inviting of our souls ? Art thou, O God !
Offended that thy weary children groan,

And wither in their anguish at thy rod,
And think it but small ill to walk alone
On this thine earth, wishing their cares away,
Yet finding them grow deadlier day by day ?

Oh, 'tis enough that the sharp solstice brings
Numb snow and frost to bite us to the heart ;
That devilish pain and sickness smite apart
Ease and keen pleasure in the face of things.
Those gifts from heaven could we take athwart
Our little eager paths, and bear the cross
Meekly ; yet they are nought to these ; hope dies
And leaves us desolate, and love is loss,
And hatred burns our bones, and mercy flies
Our sundering souls, and progress funeral
Towards the love that reigns and rules o'er all.

Our pain hath no dismissal, and our joys
But speed us to our ashes.   In life's charm
There lifts a cold, intolerable arm
Which smites the very infant at its ploys.
Our comfort wastes, and fair forms come to harm—
Naught lasts but sorrow, all things else decay,
And time is full of losing and forgetting,
Our pleasure is as iron and rusts away,
Our days are grief, and scarcely worth their setting,
Wherein there is repose and slumber deep,
And therefore are we thankful for our sleep.

We all are thankful for a little sleep,
For therein there is peace and easy death,

And solace for our sad, impatient breath.
Perchance therein we lose ourselves, and keep
Part of an ageless silence ; yet one saith
We are but born to linger and to fear,
To feel harsh fleeting time and aimless woe.
Th' inscrutable decree which brought us here
Makes myriads wretched, and shall keep them so
Till death uplifts the bars for those who wait
And yearn along the soundless gulfs of fate.

Still let us wait beneath the glorious sun,
And, be his light or strengthened or subdued,
Let light come to our eyes, for it is good
To see the small flow'rs open one by one,
And see the wild wings fleeting through the wood,
They grow and perish uncomplainingly,
And blameless live and end their blameless years,
And mayhap we are blind, and cannot see
The rainbow shining in a mist of tears ;
And mayhap we are dull, and cannot feel
The touch which strengthens and the lips which heal.

64. *From ' Tecumseh '.—Act I, Scene 2*

LEFROY

THIS region is as lavish of its flowers
   As Heaven of its primrose blooms by night.

This is the Arum, which within its root
Folds life and death ; and this the Prince's Pine,

91

CHARLES MAIR

Fadeless as love and truth—the fairest form
That ever sun-shower washed with sudden rain.
This golden cradle is the Moccasin Flower,
Wherein the Indian hunter sees his hound ;
And this dark chalice is the Pitcher-Plant,
Stored with the water of forgetfulness.
Whoever drinks of it, whose heart is pure,
Will sleep for ay 'neath foodful asphodel,
And dream of endless love.

    .   .   .   .

   There was a time on this fair continent
When all things throve in spacious peacefulness.
The prosperous forests unmolested stood,
For where the stalwart oak grew there it lived
Long ages, and then died among its kind.
The hoary pines—those ancients of the earth—
Brimful of legends of the early world,
Stood thick on their own mountains unsubdued.
And all things else illumined by the sun,
Inland or by the lifted wave, had rest.
The passionate or calm pageants of the skies
No artist drew ; but in the auburn west
Innumerable faces of fair cloud
Vanished in silent darkness with the day.
The prairie realm—vast ocean's paraphr: se—
Rich in wild grasses numberless, and flowers
Unnamed save in mute Nature's inventory,
No civilized barbarian trenched for gain.
And all that flowed was sweet and uncorrupt
The rivers and their tributary streams,

CHARLES MAIR

Undammed, wound on for ever, and gave up
Their lonely torrents to weird gulfs of sea,
And ocean wastes unshadowed by a sail.
And all the wild life of this western world
Knew not the fear of man ; yet in those woods,
And by those plenteous streams and mighty lakes,
And on stupendous steppes of peerless plain,
And in the rocky gloom of canyons deep,
Screened by the stony ribs of mountains hoar
Which steeped their snowy peaks in purging cloud,
And down the continent where tropic suns
Warmed to her very heart the mother earth,
And in the congeal'd north where silence' self
Ached with intensity of stubborn frost,
There lived a soul more wild than barbarous ;
A tameless soul—the sunburnt savage free—
Free and untainted by the greed of gain,
Great Nature's man, content with Nature's food.

EVAN M'COLL

65. *The Highland Emigrant's last Farewell*

ADIEU, my native land ; adieu,
　The banks of fair Lochfyne,
Where the first breath of life I drew,
　And would my last resign !
Swift sails the bark that wafteth me
　This night from thy loved strand ;
Oh, must it be my last of thee,
　My dear, dear fatherland !

93

EVAN M'COLL

O Scotland ! o'er the Atlantic roar
　　Though fated to depart,
Nor time nor space can e'er efface
　　Thine image from my heart.
Come weal, come woe, till life's last throe,
　　My Highland home shall seem
An Eden bright in Fancy's light,
　　A heaven in Memory's dream !

Land of the maids of matchless grace,
　　The bards of matchless song,
Land of the bold heroic race
　　That never brooked a wrong !
Long in the front of nations free
　　May Scotland proudly stand ;
Farewell to thee, farewell to thee,
　　My dear, dear fatherland !

AMOS HENRY CHANDLER

66.　　　*When Dora Died*

DREARY, dreary,
　　Fundy's mists are sweeping
Up the stricken vale of Westmoreland ;
　　Weary, weary,
Is my heart, and weeping,
While the cold waves dash upon the strand.

94

AMOS HENRY CHANDLER

Fillèd, fillèd,
Is the land with sorrow,
In loud wailing roars the angry sea;
Stillèd, stillèd,
Will they be to-morrow,
Summer notes, and murmurs on the lea.

Coldly, coldly,
Blent with autumn mists, lie
Eve's dark shadows upon the hills away;
Boldly, boldly,
Like a giant sentry,
Chapeau Dieu keeps vigil o'er the bay.

Lay me, lay me,
While the world is waking,
Down to dream on what was gone before;
Pray ye, pray ye,
Lest my heart be breaking,
God, to bring her to my side once more.

H. F. DARNELL

67. *The Maple*

ALL hail to the broad-leaved Maple,
With its fair and changeful dress!
A type of our youthful country
In its pride and loveliness.

H. F. DARNELL

Whether in Spring or Summer,
  Or in the dreary Fall,
'Mid Nature's forest children
  She 's fairest of them all.

Down sunny slopes and valleys
  Her graceful form is seen,
Her wide, umbrageous branches
  The sunburnt reaper screen ;
'Mid the dark-browed firs and cedars
  Her livelier colours shine,
Like the dawn of a brighter future
  On the settler's hut of pine.

She crowns the pleasant hill-top,
  Whispers on breezy downs,
And casts refreshing shadows
  O'er the streets of our busy towns
She gladdens the aching eyeball,
  Shelters the weary head,
And scatters her crimson glories
  On the graves of the silent dead.

When Winter's frosts are yielding
  To the sun's returning sway,
And merry groups are speeding
  To sugar-woods away ;
The sweet and welling juices,
  Which form their welcome spoil,
Tell of the teeming plenty
  Which here waits honest toil.

H. F. DARNELL

When sweet-voiced Spring, soft-breathing,
  Breaks Nature's icy sleep,
And the forest boughs are swaying
  Like the green waves of the deep ;
In her fair and budding beauty
  A fitting emblem she
Of this our land of promise,
  Of hope, of liberty.

And when her leaves, all crimson,
  Droop silently and fall,
Like drops of lifeblood welling
  From a warrior brave and tall,
They tell how fast and freely
  Would her children's blood be shed,
Ere the soil of our faith and freedom
  Should echo a foeman's tread.

Then hail to the broad-leaved Maple,
  With her fair and changeful dress !
A type of our youthful country
  In its pride and loveliness.
Whether in Spring or Summer,
  Or in the dreary Fall,
'Mid Nature's forest children
  She 's fairest of them all.

ISABELLA VALANCEY CRAWFORD

68. *March*

SHALL Thor with his hammer
  Beat on the mountain,
As on an anvil,
  A shackle and fetter ?

Shall the lame Vulcan
  Shout as he swingeth
God-like his hammer,
  And forge thee a fetter ?

Shall Jove, the Thunderer,
  Twine his swift lightnings
With his loud thunders,
  And forge thee a shackle ?

' No ! ' shouts the Titan,
  The young lion-throated ;
' Thor, Vulcan, or Jove
  Cannot shackle and bind me.'

Tell what will bind thee,
  Thou young world-shaker.
Up vault our oceans,
  Down fall our forests.

Ship masts and pillars
  Stagger and tremble,
Like reeds by the margins
  Of swift running waters.

ISABELLA VALANCEY CRAWFORD,

Men's hearts at thy roaring
  Quiver like harebells
Smitten by hailstones,
  Smitten and shaken.

' O sages and wise men !
  O bird-hearted tremblers !
Come, I will show ye
  A shackle to bind me.

I, the lion-throated,
  The shaker of mountains !
I, the invincible,
  Lasher of oceans !

Past the horizon,
  Its ring of pale azure
Past the horizon,
  Where scurry the white clouds,

There are buds and small flowers—-
  Flowers like snowflakes,
Blossoms like raindrops,
  So small and tremulous.

These in a fetter
  Shall shackle and bind me,
Shall weigh down my shouting
  With their delicate perfume ! '

ISABELLA VALANCEY CRAWFORD

But who this frail fetter
  Shall forge on an anvil,
With hammer of feather
  And anvil of velvet ?

' Past the horizon
  In the palm of a valley,
Her feet in the grasses,
  There is a maiden.

She smiles on the flowers,
  They widen and redden ;
She weeps on the flowers,
  They grow up and kiss her.

She breathes in their bosoms,
  They breathe back in odours ;
Inarticulate homage,
  Dumb adoration.

She shall wreathe them in shackles,
  Shall weave them in fetters ;
In chains shall she braid them,
  And me shall she fetter.

I, the invincible ;
  March, the earth-shaker ;
March, the sea-lifter ;
  March, the sky-render ;

March, the lion-throated.
  April, the weaver
Of delicate blossoms,
  And moulder of red buds—

Shall at the horizon,
  Its ring of pale azure,
Its scurry of white clouds,
  Meet in the sunlight.'

69.   *Love's Land*

OH, Love builds on the azure sea,
  And Love builds on the golden sand,
And Love builds on the rose-winged cloud,
  And sometimes Love builds on the land !

Oh, if Love build on sparkling sea,
  And if Love build on golden strand,
And if Love build on rosy cloud,
  To Love these are the solid land !

Oh, Love will build his lily walls,
  And Love his pearly roof will rear,
On cloud, or land, or mist, or sea—
  Love's solid land is everywhere !

70.   *Laughter*

LAUGHTER wears a lilied gown—
    She is but a simple thing;
Laughter's eyes are water-brown,
Ever glancing up and down
    Like a woodbird's restless wing.

Laughter slender is and round—
    She is but a simple thing;
And her tresses fly unbound,
And about her brow are found
    Buds that blossom by Mirth's spring.

Laughter loves to praise and play—
    She is but a simple thing—
With the children small who stray
Under hedges, where the May
    Scents and blossoms richly fling.

Laughter coyly peeps and flits—
    She is but a simple thing—
Round the flower-clad door, where sits
Maid who dimples as she knits,
    Dreaming in the rosy spring.

Laughter hath light-tripping feet—
    She is but a simple thing;
Ye may often Laughter meet
In the hayfield, gilt and sweet,
    Where the mowers jest and sing.

ISABELLA VALANCEY CRAWFORD

Laughter shakes the bounteous leaves—
   She is but a simple thing—
On the village ale-house eaves,
While the angered swallow grieves
   And the rustic revellers sing.

Laughter never comes a-nigh—
   She 's a wise though simple thing—
Where men lay them down to die;
Nor will under stormy sky
   Laughter's airy music ring.

71.   *The City Tree*

I STAND within the stony, arid town,
   I gaze for ever on the narrow street,
I hear for ever passing up and down
   The ceaseless tramp of feet.

I know no brotherhood with far-locked woods,
   Where branches bourgeon from a kindred sap,
Where o'er mossed roots, in cool, green solitudes,
   Small silver brooklets lap.

No emerald vines creep wistfully to me
   And lay their tender fingers on my bark;
High may I toss my boughs, yet never see
   Dawn's first most glorious spark.

103

ISABELLA VALANCEY CRAWFORD

When to and fro my branches wave and sway,
  Answ'ring the feeble wind that faintly calls,
They kiss no kindred boughs, but touch alway
  The stones of climbing walls.

My heart is never pierced with song of bird ;
  My leaves know nothing of that glad unrest
Which makes a flutter in the still woods heard
  When wild birds build a nest.

There never glance the eyes of violets up,
  Blue, into the deep splendour of my green ;
Nor falls the sunlight to the primrose cup
  My quivering leaves between.

Not mine, not mine to turn from soft delight
  Of woodbine breathings, honey sweet and warm ;
With kin embattled rear my glorious height
  To greet the coming storm !

Not mine to watch across the free, broad plains
  The whirl of stormy cohorts sweeping fast,
The level silver lances of great rains
  Blown onward by the blast !

Not mine the clamouring tempest to defy,
  Tossing the proud crest of my dusky leaves—
Defender of small flowers that trembling lie
  Against my barky greaves !

Not mine to watch the wild swan drift above,
  Balanced on wings that could not choose between
The wooing sky, blue as the eye of love,
  And my own tender green !

ISABELLA VALANCEY CRAWFORD

And yet my branches spread, a kingly sight,
  In the close prison of the drooping air ;
When sun-vexed noons are at their fiery height
  My shade is broad, and there

Come city toilers, who their hour of ease
  Weave out to precious seconds as they lie
Pillowed on horny hands, to hear the breeze
  Through my great branches die.

I see no flowers, but as the children race
  With noise and clamour through the dusty street,
I see the bud of many an angel face,
  I hear their merry feet.

No violets look up, but, shy and grave,
  The children pause and lift their crystal eyes
To where my emerald branches call and wave
  As to the mystic skies.

GEORGE FREDERICK CAMERON

72.   *Standing on tiptoe*

STANDING on tiptoe ever since my youth,
  Striving to grasp the future just above,
I hold at length the only future—Truth,
  And Truth is love.

I feel as one who being awhile confined
  Sees drop to dust about him all his bars ;—
The clay grows less, and, leaving it, the mind
  Dwells with the stars.

73.   '*Ah me! the mighty love*'

AH me! the mighty love that I have borne
    To thee, sweet Song! A perilous gift was it
My mother gave me that September morn
    When sorrow, song, and life were at one altar lit.

A gift more perilous than the priest's; his lore
    Is all of books and to his books extends;
And what they see and know he knows—no more,
    And with their knowing all his knowing ends.

A gift more perilous than the painter's; he
    In his divinest moments only sees
The inhumanities of colour; we
    Feel each and all the inhumanities.

74.   *What matters it*

I

WHAT reck we of the creeds of men?
    We see them—we shall see again.
What reck we of the tempest's shock?
What reck we where our anchor lock?
    On golden marl or mould—
In salt-sea flower or riven rock—
    What matter—so it hold?
106

GEORGE FREDERICK CAMERON

II

What matters it the spot we fill
    On Earth's green sod when all is said ?
When feet and hands and heart are still
    And all our pulses quieted ?
When hate or love can kill nor thrill,—
    When we are done with life, and dead ?

III

So we be haunted night nor day
    By any sin that we have sinned,
What matter where we dream away
    The ages ?—In the isles of Ind,
In Tybee, Cuba, or Cathay,
    Or in some world of winter wind ?

.IV

It may be I would wish to sleep
    Beneath the wan, white stars of June,
And hear the southern breezes creep
    Between me and the mellow moon ;
But so I do not wake to weep
    At any night or any noon,

V

And so the generous gods allow
    Repose and peace from evil dreams,
It matters little where or how
    My couch be spread :—by moving streams,
Or on some eminent mountain's brow
    Kiss'd by the morn's or sunset's beams.

GEORGE FREDERICK CAMERON

VI

For we shall rest ; the brain that planned,
  That thought or wrought or well or ill,
At gaze like Joshua's moon shall stand,
  Not working any work or will,
While eye and lip and heart and hand
  Shall all be still,—shall all be still !

75.   *True Greatness*

WHAT is true greatness ? Is 't to climb
      Above the rocks and shoals of time
To sculpture on some height sublime
        A name
To live immortal in its prime
    And flush of fame ?

What is true greatness ? Is 't to lead
  Your armèd hirelings on to bleed,
And move a terrible god, indeed,
        An hour ;
To sate your lust of gold, or greed
    Of despot power ?

What is true greatness ? Question not,
  But go to yon secluded spot
And enter yonder humble cot
        And find
A husbandman who never fought
    Or wronged his kind :

108

For whom the lips of war are dumb :
  Who loves far more than beat of drum
The cattle's low, the insect's hum
      In air :
And find true greatness in its sum
  And total there !

What is true Greatness ? 'Tis to clear
  From sorrow's eye the glistening tear :
To comfort there, to cherish here,
      To bless :
To aid, encourage, and to cheer
      Distress.

76.   *The Future*

O POET of the future ! I,
  Of the dead Present, bid thee hail !
Come forth and speak,—our speech shall die :
  Come forth and sing,—our song shall fail :
Our speech, our song fall barren,—we go by !

Our heart is weak.   In vain it swells
  And beats to bursting at the wrong :
There never sets a sun but tells
  Of weak ones trampled down by strong,
Of Truth and Justice both immured in cells.

We would aspire, but round us lies
  A maze of high desires and aims ;
Would seek a prize, but, ah ! our eyes
  Fail as we face the fallen fames
Of the great world's Olympian games.

109

GEORGE FREDERICK CAMERON

Seeing the victors vanquished, we
   Grow heartsick at the sight, and choose
To hold in fee what things there be
   Rather than in the hazard use,—
Than stake the all we have—to lose !

We all are feeble.   Still we tread
   An ever-upward sloping way ;
Deep chasms and dark are round us spread
   And bale-fires beckon us astray :
But thou shalt stand upon the mountain head.

But thou wilt look with gladdened eyes
   And see the mist of error flee,
And see the happy suns arise
   Of happier days that are to be,—
On greener, gladder earth, and clearer skies.

We, of the Morning, but behold
   The dawn afar : thine eye shalt see
The full and perfect day unfold,—
   The full and perfect day to be,
When Justice shall return as lovely as of old.

Thou, with unloosened tongue, shalt speak
   In words of subtle, silver sound,—
In words not futile now, nor weak,
   To all the nations listening round
Until they seek the light,—nor vainly seek !

GEORGE FREDERICK CAMERON

We only ask it as our share,
That, when your day-star rises clear,—
A perfect splendour in the air,—
A glory ever, far and near,—
Ye write such words—*as these of those who were !*

WILLIAM H. DRUMMOND

77.   *The Last Portage*

I'M sleepin' las' night w'en I dream a dream,
   An' a wonderful wan it seem—
For I'm off on de road I was never see,
Too long an' hard for a man lak me,
So ole he can only wait de call
Is sooner or later come to all.

De night is dark an' de portage dere
Got plaintee o' log lyin' ev'ryw'ere,
Black bush aroun' on de right an' lef',
A step from de road an' you los' you'se'f,
De moon an' de star above is gone,
But somet'ing tell me I mus' go on.

An' off in front of me as I go,
Light as a dreef of de fallin' snow,
Who is dat leetle boy dancin' dere—
Can see hees w'ite dress an' curly hair,
An' almos' touch heem, so near to me—
In an' out dere among de tree ?

111

An' den I'm hearin' a voice is say,
' Come along, fader, don't min' de way ;
De boss on de camp he sen' for you,
So your leetle boy 's goin' to tak you t'roo.
It 's easy for me, for de road I know,
'Cos I travel it many long year ago.'

An' oh ! mon Dieu ! w'en he turn hees head
I'm seein' de face of ma boy is dead—
Dead wit' de young blood in hees vein—
An' dere he 's comin' wance more again
Wit' de curly hair an' dark blue eye,
So lak de blue of de summer sky—

An' now no more for de road I care,
An' slippery log lyin' ev'ryw'ere,
De swamp on de valley de mountain too,
But climb it jus' as I used to do—
Don't stop on de road for I need no res'
So long as I see de leetle w'ite dress.

An' I foller it on, an' wance in a w'ile
He turn again wit' de baby smile,
An' say, ' Dear fader, I'm here, you see,
We're bote togedder, jus' you an' me—
Very dark to you, but to me it 's light,
De road we travel so far to-night.

' De boss on de camp w'ere I alway stay
Since ever de tam I was go away,

He welcome de poores' man dat call,
But love de leetle wan bes' of all ;
So dat 's de reason I spik for you
An' come to-night to bring you t'roo.'

Lak de young Jesu' w'en He 's here below,
De face of ma leetle son look jus' so—
Den off beyon' on de bush I see
De w'ite dress fadin' among de tree—
Was it a dream I dream las' night
Is goin' away on de mornin' light ?

78. *The Wreck of the 'Julie Plante'*

(*A Legend of Lac St. Pierre*)

ON wan dark night on Lac St. Pierre,
De win' she blow, blow, blow,
An' de crew of de wood-scow *Julie Plante*
Got scar't an' run below—
For de win' she blow lik' hurricane,
Bimeby she blow some more,
An' de scow bus' up on Lac St. Pierre
Wan arpent from de shore.

De captinne walk on de front deck,
An' walk de hin' deck too—
He call de crew from up de hole,
He call de cook also.

WILLIAM H. DRUMMOND

De cook she's name was Rosie,
　　She come from Montreal,
Was chambermaid on lumber-barge
　　On de Grande Lachine Canal.

De win' she blow from nor'-eas'-wes',
　　De sout' win' she blow too,
W'en Rosie cry, ' Mon cher captinne,
　　Mon cher, w'at I shall do ? '
De captinne t'row de beeg ankerre,
　　But still de scow she dreef :
De crew he can't pass on de shore
　　Becos' he los' hees skeef.

De night was dark lak' wan black cat,
　　De wave run high an' fas',
W'en de captinne tak' de Rosie girl
　　An' tie her to de mas'.
Den he also tak' de life-preserve,
　　An' jomp off on de lak',
An' say, ' Good-bye, my Rosie dear,
　　I go drown for your sak' ! '

Nex' mornin' very early
　　'Bout ha'f pas' two—t'ree—four—
De captinne—scow—an' de poor Rosie
　　Was corpses on de shore.
For de win' she blow lak' hurricane,
　　Bimeby she blow some more,
An' de scow bus' up on Lac St. Pierre
　　Wan arpent from de shore.

Moral

Now all good wood-scow sailor-man,
 Tak' warning by dat storm,
An' go an' marry some nice French girl
 An' leev on wan beeg farm.
De win' can blow lak' hurricane,
 An' s'pose she blow some more,
You can't get drown' on Lac St. Pierre
 So long you stay on shore.

79. *The Habitant*

DE place I get born, me, is up on de reever
 Near foot of de rapide dat 's call Cheval Blanc.
Beeg mountain behin' it, so high you can't climb it,
 An' whole place she 's mebbe two honder arpent.

De fader of me, he was habitant farmer,
 Ma gran'fader too, an' hees fader also,
Dey don't mak' no monee, but dat isn't fonny
 For it 's not easy get ev'ryt'ing, you mus' know.

All de sam' dere is somet'ing dey got ev'ry boddy,
 Dat 's plaintee good healt', wat de monee can't geev,
So I'm workin' away dere, an' happy for stay dere
 On farm by de reever, so long I was leev.

Oh ! dat was de place w'en de spring tam she 's comin',
 W'en snow go away, an' de sky is all blue—
W'en ice lef' de water, an sun is get hotter,
 An back on de medder is sing de gou-glou—

WILLIAM H. DRUMMOND

W'en small sheep is firs' comin' out on de pasture,
 Deir nice leetle tail stickin' up on deir back,
Dey ronne wit' deir moder, an' play wit' each oder,
 An' jomp all de tam jus' de sam' dey was crack—

An' ole cow also, she 's glad winter is over,
 So she kick herse'f up, an' start off on de race
Wit' de two-year-ole heifer, dat 's purty soon lef' her,
 W'y ev'ryt'ing 's crazee all over de place !

An' down on de reever de wil' duck is quackin',
 Along by de shore leetle san' piper ronne—
De bullfrog he 's gr-rompin' an' doré is jompin'—
 Dey all got deir own way for mak' it de fonne.

But spring 's in beeg hurry, and don't stay long wit' us,
 An' firs' t'ing we know, she go off till nex' year ;
Den bee commence hummin', for summer is comin',
 An' purty soon corn 's gettin' ripe on de ear.

Dat 's very nice tam for wake up on de mornin'
 An' lissen de rossignol sing ev'ry place,
Feel sout' win' a-blowin', see clover a-growin',
 An' all de worl' laughin' itself on de face.

Mos' ev'ry day raf' it is pass on de rapide,
 De voyageur singin' some ole chanson
'Bout girl down de reever—too bad dey mus' leave her,
 But comin' back soon wit' beaucoup d'argent.

WILLIAM H. DRUMMOND

An' den w'en de fall an de winter come roun' us,
   An' bird of de summer is all fly away,
W'en mebbe she 's snowin', an' nort' win' is blowin',
   An' night is mos' t'ree tam so long as de day.

You t'ink it was bodder de habitant farmer?
   Not at all—he is happy an' feel satisfy,
An' cole may las' good w'ile, so long as de wood pile
   Is ready for burn on de stove by an' bye.

W'en I got plaintee hay put away on de stable
   So de sheep an' de cow, dey got no chance to freeze,
An' de hen all togedder—I don't min' de wedder—
   De nort' win' may blow jus' so moche as she please.

An' some cole winter night how I wish you can see us,
   W'en I smoke on de pipe, an' de ole woman sew
By de stove of Tree Reever—ma wife's fader geeve her
   On day we get marry, dat 's long tam ago.

De boy an' de girl, dey was readin' it's lesson,
   De cat on de corner she 's bite heem de pup,
Ole ' Carleau ', he 's snorin', an' beeg stove is roarin'
   So loud dat I'm scare purty soon she bus' up.

Philomene—dat 's de oldes'—is sit on de winder,
   An' kip jus' so quiet lak wan leetle mouse,
She say de more finer moon never was shiner—
   Very fonny, for moon isn't dat side de house.

But purty soon den, we hear foot on de outside,
　　An' some wan is place it hees han' on de latch :
Dat 's Isidore Goulay, las' fall on de Brulé
　　He 's tak' it firs' prize on de grand ploughin' match.

Ha! ha! Philomene!—dat was smart trick you play us ;
　　Come help de young feller tak' snow from hees neck :
Dere 's not'ing for hinder you come off de winder
　　W'en moon you was look for is come, I expec'.

Isidore, he is tole us de news on de parish
　　'Bout hees Lajeunesse Colt—travel two forty, sure,
'Bout Jeremie Choquette, come back from Woonsocket,
　　An' t'ree new leetle twin on Madam Vaillancour' !

But nine o'clock strike, an' de chil'ren is sleepy,
　　Mese'f an' ole woman can't stay up no more ;
So alone by de fire—'cos dey say dey ain't tire—
　　We lef' Philomene an' de young Isidore.

I s'pose dey be talkin' beeg lot on de kitchen
　　'Bout all de nice moon dey was see on de sky ;
For Philomene 's takin' long tam get awaken
　　Nex' day, she 's so sleepy on bote of de eye.

Dat 's wan of dem t'ings, ev'ry tam on de fashion,
　　An' 'bout nices' t'ing dat was never be seen.
Got not'ing for say me—I spark it sam' way me
　　W'en I go see de moder, ma girl Philomene.

118

WILLIAM H. DRUMMOND

We leev very quiet 'way back on de contree,
   Don't put on sam' style lak' de big village ;
W'en we don't get de monee you t'ink dat is fonny
   An' mak' plaintee sport on de Bottes Sauvages.

But I tole you—dat 's true—I don't go on de city
   If you geev de fine house an' beaucoup d'argent—
I rader be stay me, an' spen' de las' day me
   On de farm by de rapide dat 's call Cheval Blanc.

80.   *Johnnie Courteau*

JOHNNIE COURTEAU of de mountain,
   Johnnie Courteau of de hill—
Dat was de boy can shoot de gun,
Dat was de boy can jomp an' run,
   An' it 's not very offen you ketch heem still—
                 Johnnie Courteau !

Ax dem along de reever,
   Ax dem along de shore,
Who was mos' bes' fightin' man
From Managance to Shaw-in-i-gan ?
   De place w'ere de great beeg rapide roar—
                 Johnnie Courteau !

Sam' t'ing on ev'ry shaintee
   Up on de Mekinac :
Who was de man can walk de log,
W'en w'ole of de reever she 's black wit' fog,
   An' carry de beeges' load on hees back ?
                 Johnnie Courteau !

WILLIAM H. DRUMMOND

On de rapide you want to see heem
 If de raf' she 's swingin' roun',
An' he 's yellin', ' Hooraw Bateese ! good man ! '
W'y de oar come double on hees han'
 W'en he 's makin' dat raf' go flyin' down—
      Johnnie Courteau !

An' Tête de Boule chief can tole you
 De feller w'at save hees life,
W'en beeg moose ketch heem up a tree,
Who 's shootin' dat moose on de head, sapree !
 An' den run off wit' hees Injun wife ?
      Johnnie Courteau !

An' he only have pike pole wit' heem
 On Lac a la Tortue,
W'en he meet de bear comin' down de hill,
But de bear very soon is get hees fill !
 An' he sole dat skin for ten dollar too—
      Johnnie Courteau !

Oh, he never was scare for not'ing
 Lak de ole coureurs de bois,
But w'en he 's gettin' hees winter pay
De bes' t'ing sure is kip out de way ;
 For he 's goin' right off on de Hip Hooraw !
      Johnnie Courteau !

Den pullin' hees sash aroun' heem
 He dance on hees botte sauvage,

An' shout, ' All aboar' if you want to fight ! '
Wall ! you never can see de finer sight
  W'en he go lak dat on de w'ole village !
                Johnnie Courteau !

But Johnnie Courteau get marry
  On Philomene Beaurepaire :
She 's nice leetle girl was run de school
On w'at you call Parish of Sainte Ursule,
  An' he see her off on de pique-nique dere—
                Johnnie Courteau !

Den somet'ing come over Johnnie
  W'en he marry on Philomene,
For he stay on de farm de w'ole year roun',
He chop de wood an' he plough de groun',
  An' he 's quieter feller was never seen—
                Johnnie Courteau !

An' ev'ry wan feel astonish,
  From La Tuque to Shaw-in-i-gan,
W'en dey hear de news was goin' aroun',
Along on de reever up an' down,
  How wan leetle woman boss dat beeg man—
                Johnnie Courteau !

He never come out on de evening
No matter de hard we try,
'Cos he stay on de kitchen an' sing hees song :
  ' A la claire fontaine,
    M'en allant promener,

J'ai trouvé l'eau si belle
Que je m'y suis baigner !
Il y a longtemps que je t'aime,
Jamais je ne t'oublierai.'
Rockin' de cradle de w'ole night long,
Till baby 's asleep on de sweet bimeby—
                          Johnnie Courteau !

An' de house, wall ! I wish you see it :.
  De place she 's so nice an' clean
Mus' wipe your foot on de outside door,
You're dead man sure if you spit on de floor,
  An' he never say not'ing on Philomene—
                          Johnnie Courteau !

An' Philomene watch de monee
  An' put it all safe away
On very good place ; I dunno w'ere,
But anyhow nobody see it dere,
  So she 's buyin' new farm de noder day—
                          Madame Courteau !

81.   *Little Bateese*

YOU bad leetle boy, not moche you care
  How busy you're kipin' your poor gran' père
    Tryin' to stop you ev'ry day
    Chasin' de hen aroun' de hay—
    W'y don't you geev' dem a chance to lay ?
                          Leetle Bateese !

WILLIAM H. DRUMMOND

Off on de fiel' you foller de plough,
Den w'en you're tire you scare de cow,
    Sickin' de dog till dey jomp de wall,
    So de milk ain't good for not'ing at all—
    An' you're only five an' a half dis fall,
                        Leetle Bateese !

Too sleepy for sayin' de prayer to night ?
Never min', I s'pose it'll be all right.
    Say dem to-morrow—ah ! dere he go !
    Fas' asleep in a minute or so—
    An' he'll stay lak dat till de rooster crow,
                        Leetle Bateese !

Den wake us up right away tout de suite
Lookin' for somet'ing more to eat,
    Makin' me t'ink of dem long leg crane—
    Soon as dey swaller, dey start again ;
    I wonder your stomach don't get no pain,
                        Leetle Bateese !

But see heem now lyin' dere in bed,
Look at de arm onderneat' hees head ;
    If he grow like dat till he 's twenty year
    I bet he'll be stronger dan Louis Cyr,
    An' beat all de voyageurs leevin' here,
                        Leetle Bateese !

Jus' feel de muscle along hees back,
Won't geev' heem moche bodder for carry pack

On de long portage, any size canoe ;
Dere 's not many t'ing dat boy won't do,
For he 's got double-joint on hees body too,
     Leetle Bateese !

But leetle Bateese ! please don't forget
We rader you're stayin' de small boy yet ;
 So chase de chicken an' mak' dem scare,
 An' do w'at you lak wit' your ole gran' père,
 For w'en you're beeg feller he won't be dere—
     Leetle Bateese !

82.   *Little Lac Grenier*

     (Gren-Yay)

LEETLE Lac Grenier, she 's all alone,
 Right on de mountain top,
But cloud sweepin' by, will fin' tam to stop
No matter how quickly he want to go,
So he'll kiss leetle Grenier down below.

Leetle Lac Grenier, she 's all alone,
Up on de mountain high ;
But she never feel lonesome, 'cos for w'y ?
So soon as de winter was gone away
De bird come an' sing to her ev'ry day.

WILLIAM H. DRUMMOND

Leetle Lac Grenier, she 's all alone,
Back on de mountain dere,
But de pine-tree an' spruce stan' ev'rywhere
Along by de shore, an' mak' her warm,
For dey kip off de win' an' de winter storm.

Leetle Lac Grenier, she 's all alone,
No broder, no sister near,
But de swallow will fly, an' de beeg moose deer,
An' caribou too, will go long way
To drink de sweet water of Lac Grenier.

Leetle Lac Grenier, I see you now,
Onder de roof of Spring ;
Ma canoe 's afloat, an' de robin sing,
De lily 's beginnin' her summer dress,
An' trout 's wakin' up from hees long long res'

Leetle Lac Grenier, I'm happy now,
Out on de ole canoe,
For I'm all alone, ma chère, wit' you,
An' if only a nice light rod I had
I'd try dat fish near de lily pad !

Leetle Lac Grenier, oh ! let me go.
Don't spik no more,
For your voice is strong lak de rapid's roar,
An' you know you'se'f I'm too far away
For visit you now—leetle Lac Grenier !

WILLIAM McLENNAN

83. *Day*

THE Day hath burst exuberant from out the pearl-
    grey Dawn.
She flings aside her crimson robe behind the golden
    hills,
And comes in all her nakedness, her very veil with-
    drawn,
In glory so effulgent that it troubles as it thrills.

The cicada is screaming high her paean to the heat,
The tender morning flowers have hid their faces from
    the glare,
As dancing through the swooning land Day reels with
    burning feet,
The red hibiscus flaunting in her iridescent hair.

84. *Malbrouck*

(*Translation of an old Chanson*)

MALBROUCK has gone a-fighting,
    Mironton, mironton, mirontaine,
Malbrouck has gone a-fighting,
But when will he return ?

Perchance he'll come at Easter,
Or else at Trinity Term.

WILLIAM McLENNAN

But Trinity Term is over
And Malbrouck comes not yet.

My Lady climbs her watch-tower
As high as she can get.

She sees her page approaching
All clad in sable hue :

' Ah, page, brave page, what tidings
From my true lord bring you ? '

' The news I bring, fair Lady,
Will make your tears run down ;

' Put off your rose-red dress so fine
And doff your satin gown.

' Monsieur Malbrouck is dead, alas !
And buried too, for ay ;

' I saw four officers who bore
His mighty corse away.

' One bore his cuirass, and his friend
His shield of iron wrought ;

' The third his mighty sabre bore,
And the fourth—he carried nought.

' And at the corners of his tomb
They planted rose-marie ;

' And from their tops the nightingale
Rings out her carol free.

WILLIAM McLENNAN

'We saw, above the laurels,
His soul fly forth amain;

'And each one fell upon his face
And then rose up again.

'And so we sang the glories
For which great Malbrouck bled;

'And when the whole was ended
Each one went off to bed.

'I say no more, my Lady,
  Mironton, mironton, mirontaine,
I say no more, my Lady,
As nought more can be said.'

85. *En roulant ma Boule*

(*Translation of an old Chanson*)

BEHIND the Manor lies the mere,
  En roulant ma boule;
Three ducks bathe in its water clear,
  En roulant ma boule.

> *Rouli, roulant, ma boule roulant,*
> *En roulant ma boule, roulant,*
> *En roulant ma boule.*

Three fairy ducks swim without fear:
The Prince goes hunting far and near.

The Prince at last draws near the lake:
He bears his gun of magic make.

128

WILLIAM McLENNAN

With magic gun of silver bright,
He sights the Black but kills the White.

He sights the Black but kills the White :
Ah ! cruel Prince, my heart you smite.

Ah ! cruel Prince, my heart you break,
In killing thus my snow white Drake.

My snow-white Drake, my Love, my King ;
The crimson life-blood stains his wing.

His life-blood falls in rubies bright,
His diamond eyes have lost their light.

The cruel ball has found its quest,
His golden bill sinks on his breast.

His golden bill sinks on his breast,
His plumes go floating East and West.

Far, far they're borne to distant lands,
Till gathered by fair maidens' hands ;

Till gathered by fair maidens' hands,
And form at last a soldier's bed.

And form at last a soldier's bed,
   En roulant ma boule.
Sweet refuge for the wanderer's head,
   En roulant ma boule.

    Rouli, roulant, ma boule roulant,
    En roulant ma boule, roulant,
    En roulant ma boule.

EDWARD B. BROWNLOW

86.   *The Song of Orpheus*

PERSEPHONE ! Persephone !
  Give back my lost delight to me !
By thy great love for thy great lord,
By each sweet thought for him adored,
By love that thrills and love that fills
Thy heart as with a thousand rills
Of joy, break down his frozen breast
And lull his vengeful mood to rest,
Till mighty Pluto joyfully
Shall, from his very love for thee,
Give back my soul's delight to me—
      Eurydice ! Eurydice !

Persephone ! Persephone !
Recall thy lord's great love for thee,
When in sweet Enna's golden meads
Thou heard'st that rustling of the reeds,
And in thy hands the love-crushed flowers
Were grasped with fear, as from earth's bowers
He strained thee to his mighty breast,
And bore thee, senseless, to the West,
Beyond the opalescent sea
That nightly sings its song of thee ;
Give back my soul's delight to me—
      Eurydice ! Eurydice !

130

EDWARD B. BROWNLOW

Persephone ! Persephone !
Mark how thy lord yet frowns on me,
Behold the tightening of his lip—
Kiss, kiss his mouth lest there may slip
One word of doom to dash my hope :
Bend down on him thine eyes, and cope
With love the gleams that in them shine,
The while I summon to me, mine ;
Break, break, by love and memory
The bond of Hades, set me free
Her soul, that is the soul of me—
Eurydice ! Eurydice !

Persephone ! Persephone !
Clasp him so close he may not see ;
Look deep into his soul with love
That from thine eyes he shall not move
His own ;—ah ! thus I gazed on her
That night and heard no serpent stir,
For love, once thralling all the mind,
Makes all the little senses blind ;
'Tis well ! he drinks love's alchemy !
Where'er in Hades thou may'st be—
Come back ! my love ! come back to me,
Eurydice ! Eurydice !

Persephone ! Persephone !
Lull him with love that unto me
No thought may leap with sudden ire,
And steal again my heart's desire

EDWARD B. BROWNLOW

When she shall come.   Ye gods ! that light,
It shone when on that fatal night
The daemons took her from my side ;
'Tis she ! they bring her back, my bride !
Let Pluto wake ! let Jove decree !
Myself—my soul—come back to me
My joy in life and death to be—
      Eurydice ! Eurydice !

      Persephone ! Persephone !
A moment more and we are free ;
I feel the breath of outer air,
I see the upper stars so fair,
I hear the lapping of salt waves,
I see the light of day that saves,
I feel the pulsing heart-throbs run
Through her fair limbs, I watch the sun
Uprising in her eyes—and see !
Its living light thrills into me ;
She has come back—come back to me !—
      Eurydice ! Eurydice !

EDWARD W. THOMSON

87.   *In June*

The Canadian Rossignol on Mount Royal

PRONE where maples widely spread
  I watch the far blue overhead,
Where little fine-spun clouds arise
From naught to naught before my eyes ;

132

EDWARD W. THOMSON

Within the shade a pleasant rout
Of dallying zephyrs steal about ;
Lazily as moves the day
Odours float and faint away
From roses yellow, red, and white,
That prank yon garden with delight ;
Round which the locust blossoms swing,
And some late lilacs droop for spring.
Anon swells up a dubious breeze
Stirring the half reluctant trees,
Then, rising to a mimic gale,
Ruffles the massy oak to pale
Till, spent its sudden force, once more
The zephyrs come that went before ;
Now silvery poplars shivering stand,
And languid lindens waver bland,
Hemlock traceries scarcely stir,
All the pines of summer purr ;
Hovering butterflies I see,
Full of business shoots the bee,
Straight to yon valley is his flight
Where solemn marbles crowd so white.
Half hid in the grasses there
Red-breast thrushes jump and stare,
Sparrows flutter up like leaves
Tossed upon the wind in sheaves.
Curve-winged swallows slant and slide
O'er the graves that stretch so wide,
Steady crows go labouring by—
Ha ! the Rossignol is nigh !

EDWARD W. THOMSON

Rossignol, why will you sing
Though lost the lovely world of spring ?
'Twas well that then your roulades rang
Of joy, despite of every pang,
But now the sweet, the bliss is gone—
  Nay, now the summer joy is on,
  And lo, the foliage and the bloom,
  The fuller life the bluer room,
  'Twas this the sweet spring promised me.
O bird, and can you sing so free ?
And will you sing when summer goes
And leaves turn brown and dies the rose ?
  Oh, then how brave shall autumn dress
  The maple out with gorgeousness !
  And red-cheeked apples deck the green,
  And corn wave tall its yellow sheen.
But, bird, bethink you well, I pray,
Then marches winter on his way.
  Ah, winter—yes, ah, yes—but still
  Hark ! sweetly chimes the summer rill,
  And joy is here and life is strong,
  And love still calls upon my song.

No, Rossignol, sing not that strain,
Triumphant 'spite of all the pain,—
She cannot hear you, Rossignol,
She does not pause and flush, your thrall.
She does not raise that slender hand
And, poised lips parted, understand

EDWARD W. THOMSON

What you are telling of the years,
Her brown eyes soft with happy tears,—
She does not hear a note of all.
Ah, Rossignol, ah, Rossignol !
But skies are blue and flowers bloom,
And roses breathe the old perfume,
And here the murmuring of the trees
In all of lovelier mysteries ;—
And maybe now she hears my song
Pouring the summer hills along,
Listens with joy that still to thee
Remain the summertime and me.

WILLIAM D. LIGHTHALL

88.   *The Confused Dawn*

Young Man

WHAT are the Vision and the Cry
    That haunt the new Car dian soul ?
Dim grandeur spreads, we know not why,
    O'er mountain, forest, tree, and knoll,
And murmurs indistinctly fly—
Some magic moment sure is nigh.
    O Seer, the curtain roll !

Seer

The Vision, mortal, it is this—
    Dead mountain, forest, knoll, and tree,
Awaken all endued with bliss,
    A native land—O think ! to be

WILLIAM D. LIGHTHALL

Thy native land—and, ne'er amiss,
Its smile shall like a lover's kiss,
    From henceforth seem to thee.

The Cry thou couldst not understand,
    Which runs through that new realm of light,
From Breton's to Vancouver's strand,
    O'er many a lovely landscape bright,
It is their waking utterance grand,
The great refrain, ' A Native Land ! '
    Thine be the ear, the sight.

89.   *The Battle of La Prairie*

(A Ballad of 1691)

I

THAT was a brave old epoch,
    Our age of chivalry,
When the Briton met the Frenchman
    At the Fight of La Prairie ;
And the manhood of New England,
    And the Netherlanders true,
And Mohawks sworn, gave battle
    To the Bourbon's lilied blue.

II

That was a brave old Governor,
    Who gathered his array,
And stood to meet he knew not what,
    On that alarming day.
136

WILLIAM D. LIGHTHALL

Eight hundred, against rumours vast
　　That filled the wild wood's gloom,
With all New England's flower of youth,
　　Fierce for New France's doom.

III

And the brave old scarce three hundred !
　　Theirs should in truth be fame ;
Borne down the savage Richelieu
　　On what emprise they came !
Your hearts are great enough, O few ;
　　Only your numbers fail !
New France asks more for conquerors,
　　All glorious though your tale.

IV

It was a brave old battle
　　That surged around the fort,
When D'Hosta fell in charging,
　　And 'twas deadly strife and short ;
When in the very quarters
　　They contested face and hand,
And many a goodly fellow
　　Crimsoned yon La Prairie sand.

V

And those were brave old orders
　　The colonel gave to meet
That forest force, with trees entrenched,
　　Opposing the retreat ;

WILLIAM D. LIGHTHALL

' De Callières' strength behind us,
 And beyond 's your Richelieu ;
We must go straightforth at them ;
 There is nothing else to do.'

VI

And then the brave old story comes,
 Of Schuyler and Valrennes,
When ' Fight ! ' the British colonel called,
 Encouraging his men,
' For the Protestant Religion,
 And the honour of our King ! '—
' Sir, I am here to answer you ! '
 Valrennes cried, forth stepping.

VII

Were those not brave old races ?
 Well, here they still abide ;
And yours is one or other,
 And the second 's at your side.
So when you hear your brother say,
 ' Some loyal deed I'll do ; '
Like old Valrennes be ready with,
 ' I'm here to answer you ! '

WILLIAM D. LIGHTHALL

90.   *Montreal*

REIGN on, majestic Ville-Marie !
   Spread wide thy ample robes of state ;
  The heralds cry that thou art great,
And proud are thy young sons of thee
Mistress of half a continent,
   Thou risest from thy girlhood's rest ;
  We see thee conscious heave thy breast
And feel thy rank and thy descent.

Sprung of the saint and chevalier !
   And with the Scarlet Tunic wed !
   Mount Royal's crown upon thy head ;
And past thy footstool, broad and clear,
St. Lawrence sweeping to the sea ;
Reign on, majestic Ville-Marie !

91.   *' Eben Picken, Bookseller '*

PICKEN of Beaver Hall, what modest hand,
  Or thoughtless, wrote thy sign ? ' Bookseller '
    thou,
Forsooth ! Though goodly word it be, and graced
By learning, honour, men of fair repute.
Not this the operation of thy days,
No barter thought, no views of bank account,
Silver and bills, profit, advertisement ;
Not this thy avocation—but to lead

WILLIAM D. LIGHTHALL

The novice soul along the temple path
To the hid shrine, the thirsty heart to find
Some quenching draft, the world's delights to lift
Before the unthinking.   Gentle Levite thou
Of Art and Wisdom and Humanity
And the inclusive ONE.   To thee we fare
To meet the souls of poets, and converse
With sages, known or called from quarters strange
By thy skilled wand.   That unpretentious door
Leads where wise Plato visits still the earth,
And Shakespeare calls his airy host to view :
Ah, what a world is there, delectable,
Serene, of perfect grace, the land of Thought !
There in their kingly ranks the Masters walk
By crocus-edged Cephisus' sleepless stream
Along the cypress paths.   There Socrates,
Virgil and Zarathustra, Francis mild,
Memline and Angelo and Angelico,
The bard of Faust and he of Paradise—
Heroes and saints innumerable appear,
While in their converse he who will takes part
And thou art friend and guide.   Assuredly
'Tis blessed to be thus amid a world
Mad after fruit of ashes, running fast
Because the rest are running, blind and deaf
And needing quiet voices like to thine.

COLIN A. SCOTT

92.   *The Poet*

SWEET words waiting since the early times,
　For him have tarried.
For him they rush into his rhymes
　For ever married.

Ambassador of birds and bees,
　He knows their meaning :
The spokesman of the tongueless trees,
　Grey grown, or greening ;

And even my heart he reads aright,
　Through magic seeming ;
At last my lips can utter quite
　My soul's deep dreaming.

CHARLES G. D. ROBERTS

93.   *Canada*

O CHILD of nations, giant-limbed,
　Who stand'st among the nations now,
Unheeded, unadorned, unhymned,
　With unanointed brow,—

How long the ignoble sloth, how long
　The trust in greatness not thine own ?
Surely the lion's brood is strong
　To front the world alone !

CHARLES G. D. ROBERTS

How long the indolence, ere thou dare
   Achieve thy destiny, seize thy fame—
Ere our proud eyes behold thee bear
   A nation's franchise, nation's name ?

The Saxon force, the Celtic fire,
   These are thy Manhood's heritage !
Why rest with babes and slaves ? Seek higher
   The place of race and age.

I see to every wind unfurled
   The flag that bears the Maple-Wreath ;
Thy swift keels furrow round the world
   Its blood-red folds beneath ;

Thy swift keels cleave the furthest seas ;
   Thy white sails swell with alien gales ;
To stream on each remotest breeze
   The black smoke of thy pipes exhales.

O Falterer, let thy past convince
   Thy future,—all the growth, the gain,
The fame since Cartier knew thee, since
   Thy shores beheld Champlain !

Montcalm and Wolfe ! Wolfe and Montcalm !
   Quebec, thy storied citadel
Attest in burning song and psalm
   How here thy heroes fell !

CHARLES G. D. ROBERTS

O thou that bor'st the battle's brunt
  At Queenston and at Lundy's Lane,
On whose scant ranks but iron front
  The battle broke in vain !

Whose was the danger, whose the day,
  From whose triumphant throats the cheers,
At Chrysler's Farm, at Chateauguay,
  Storming like clarion-bursts our ears ?

On soft Pacific slopes, beside
  Strange floods that Northward rave and fall,
Where chafes Acadia's chainless tide,
  Thy sons await thy call.

They await ; but some in exile, some
  With strangers housed, in stranger lands.
And some Canadian lips are dumb
  Beneath Egyptian sands.

O mystic Nile ! Thy secret yields
  Before us ; thy most ancient dreams
Are mixed with far Canadian fields
  And murmur of Canadian streams.

But thou, my Country, dream not thou !
  Wake, and behold how night is done ;
How on thy breast, and o'er thy brow,
  Bursts the uprising Sun !

CHARLES G. D. ROBERTS

94.   *Grey Rocks and Greyer Sea*

GREY rocks, and greyer sea,
  And surf along the shore—
And in my heart a name
  My lips shall speak no more.

The high and lonely hills
  Endure the darkening year—
And in my heart endure
  A memory and a tear.

Across the tide a sail
  That tosses and is gone—
And in my heart the kiss
  That longing dreams upon.

Grey rocks, and greyer sea,
  And surf along the shore—
And in my heart the face
  That I shall see no more.

CHARLES G. D. ROBERTS

95.   *The Sower*

A BROWN sad-coloured hill-side, where the soil,
  Fresh from the frequent harrow, deep and fine,
  Lies bare ; no break in the remote sky-line,
Save where a flock of pigeons streams aloft,
Startled from feed in some low-lying croft,
  Or far-off spires with yellow of sunset shine ;
  And here the Sower, unwittingly divine,
Exerts the silent forethought of his toil.

Alone he treads the glebe, his measured stride
  Dumb in the yielding soil ; and though small joy
Dwell in his heavy face, as spreads the blind
Pale grain from his dispensing palm aside,
  This plodding churl grows great in his employ ;—
Godlike, he makes provision for mankind.

96.   *Epitaph for a Sailor buried Ashore*

H E, who, but yesterday would roam
  Careless as clouds and currents range,
In homeless wandering most at home,
  Inhabiter of change :

Who wooed the West to win the East,
  And named the stars of North and South,
And felt the zest of Freedom's feast
  Familiar in his mouth :

Who found a faith in stranger speech,
   And fellowship in foreign hands,
And had within his eager reach
   The relish of all lands—

How circumscribed a plot of earth
   Keeps now his restless footsteps still,
Whose wish was wide as ocean's girth,
   Whose will the water's will !

97.   *Marsyas*

A LITTLE grey hill-glade, close-turfed, withdrawn
   Beyond resort or heed of trafficking feet,
Ringed round with slim trunks of the mountain ash.
Through the slim trunks and scarlet bunches flash—
Beneath the clear chill glitterings of the dawn—
Far off, the crest, where down the rosy shore
The Pontic surges beat.
The plains lie dim below. The thin airs wash
The circuit of the autumn-coloured hills,
And this high glade, whereon
The satyr pipes, who soon shall pipe no more.
He sits against the beech-tree's mighty bole,—
He leans, and with persuasive breathing fills
The happy shadows of the slant-set lawn.
The goat-feet fold beneath a gnarled root ;
And sweet, and sweet the note that steals and thrills
From slender stops of that shy flute.
Then to the goat-feet comes the wide-eyed fawn
Hearkening ; the rabbits fringe the glade, and lay

Their long ears to the sound ;
In the pale boughs the partridge gather round,
And quaint hern from the sea-green river reeds ;
The wild ram halts upon a rocky horn
O'erhanging ; and, unmindful of his prey,
The leopard steals with narrowed lids to lay
His spotted length along the ground.
The thin airs wash, the thin clouds wander by,
And those hushed listeners move not.   All the morn
He pipes, soft-swaying, and with half-shut eye,
In rapt content of utterance,—
                              Nor heeds
The young god standing in his branchy place,
The languor on his lips, and in his face,
Divinely inaccessible, the scorn.

98.   *A Song of Growth*

IN the heart of a man
    Is a thought upfurled :
Reached its full span
    It will shake the world,—
And to one high thought
Is a whole race wrought.

Not with vain noise
    The great work grows,
Nor with foolish voice,—
    But in repose ;
Not in the rush,
But in the hush !

CHARLES G. D. ROBERTS

From the cogent lash
　　Of the cloud-herd wind
The low clouds dash,
　　Blown headlong, blind ;
But beyond, the great blue
Looks moveless through.

O'er the loud world sweep
　　The scourge and the rod :
But in deep beyond deep
　　Is the stillness of God,—
At the fountains of Life
No cry, no strife !

99.　　　　*The Clearing*

STUMPS, and harsh rocks, and prostrate trunks all
　　charred,
　　And gnarled roots naked to the sun and rain,—
　　They seem in their grim stillness to complain,
And by their plaint the evening peace is jarred.
These ragged acres fire and the axe have scarred,
　　And many summers not assuaged their pain.
　　In vain the pink and saffron light, in vain
The pale dew on the hillocks stripped and marred.

But here and there the waste is touched with cheer
　　Where spreads the fire-weed like a crimson flood,
And venturous plumes of golden-rod appear ;
And round the blackened fence the great boughs lear
　　With comfort ; and across the solitude
The hermit's holy transport peals serene.

148

CHARLES G. D. ROBERTS

100.   *The Potato Harvest*

A HIGH bare field, brown from the plough, and
    borne
  Aslant from sunset ; amber wastes of sky
  Washing the ridge ; a clamour of crows that fly
In from the wide flats where the spent tides mourn
To yon their rocking roosts in pines wind-torn ;
  A line of grey snake-fence, that zigzags by
  A pond, and cattle ; from the homestead nigh
The long deep summonings of the supper horn.

Black on the ridge, against that lonely flush,
  A cart, and stoop-necked oxen ; ranged beside,
    Some barrels ; and the day-worn harvest folk,
Here emptying their baskets, jar the hush
  With hollow thunders ; down the dusk hill-side
    Lumbers the wain ; and day fades out like smoke.

101.   *Tantramar Revisited*

S UMMERS and summers have come, and gone with
    the flight of the swallow ;
Sunshine and thunder have been, storm and winter
    and frost ;
Many and many a sorrow has all but died from
    remembrance,
Many a dream of joy fall'n in the shadow of pain.
Hands of chance and change have marred, or moulded,
    or broken,

Busy with spirit or flesh, all I most have adored ;
Even the bosom of earth is strewn with heavier
    shadows,—
Only in these green hills, aslant to the sea, no change.
Here, where the road that has climbed from the inland
    valleys and woodlands
Dips from the hilltops down, straight to the base of
    the hills,—
Here, from my vantage ground, I can see the scattering
    houses,
Stained with time, set warm in orchards and meadows
    and wheat
Dotting the broad, bright slopes outspread to south-
    ward and eastward,
Windswept all day long, blown by the south-east wind.
Skirting the sun-bright uplands stretches a riband of
    meadow,
Shorn of the labouring grass, bulwarked well from the
    sea,
Fenced on its seaward border with long clay dikes
    from the turbid
Surge and flow of the tides vexing the Westmoreland
    shores.
`Yonder, towards the left, lie broad the Westmoreland
    marshes,—
Miles on miles they extend, level and grassy, and dim,
Clear from the long red sweep of flats to the sky in
    the distance,
Save for the outlying heights, green-rampired Cumber-
    land Point ;

CHARLES G. D. ROBERTS

Miles on miles outrolled, and the river-channels divide
    them,—
Miles on miles of green, barred by the hurtling gusts.

Miles on miles beyond the tawny bay is Minudie.
There are the low blue hills ; villages gleam at their
    feet.
Nearer a white sail shines across the water, and nearer
Still are the slim grey masts of fishing-boats dry on the
    flats.
Ah ! how well I remember those wide red flats, above
    tide-mark,
Pale with scurf of the salt, seamed and baked in the sun !
Well I remember the piles of blocks and ropes, and the
    net-reels
Wound with the beaded nets, dripping and dark from
    the sea !
Now at this season the nets are unwound ; they hang
    from the rafters
Over the fresh-stowed hay in upland barns, and the
    wind
Blows all day through the chinks, with the streaks of
    sunlight, and sways them
Softly at will ; or they lie heaped in the gloom of a loft.
Now at this season the reels are empty and idle ; I see
    them
Over the lines of the dikes, over the gossiping grass.
Now at this season they swing in the long strong wind,
    through the lonesome
Golden afternoon, shunned by the foraging gulls.

CHARLES G. D. ROBERTS

Near about sunset the crane will journey homeward
    above them ;
Round them, under the moon, all the calm night long,
Winnowing soft grey wings of marsh-owls wander and
    wander,
Now to the broad lit marsh, now to the dusk of the
    dike.
Soon, through their dew-wet frames, in the live keen
    freshness of morning,
Out of the teeth of the dawn blows back the awakening
    wind.
Then, as the blue day mounts, and the low-shot shafts
    of the sunlight
Glance from the tide to the shore, gossamers jewelled
    with dew
Sparkle and wave, where late sea-spoiling fathoms of
    drift-net,
Myriad-meshed, uploomed sombrely over the land.

Well I remember it all. The salt raw scent of the
    margin ;
While, with men at the windlass, groaned each reel,
    and the net,
Surging in ponderous lengths, uprose and coiled in its
    station ;
Then each man to his home,—well I remember it all !

Yet, as I sit and watch, this present peace of the land-
    scape,—
Stranded boats, these reels empty and idle, the hush,

CHARLES G. D. ROBERTS

One grey hawk slow-wheeling above yon cluster of
    haystacks,
More than the old-time stir this stillness welcomes me
    home.

Ah, the old-time stir, how once it stung me with
    rapture !
Old-time sweetness, the winds freighted with honey
    and salt !
Yet will I stay my steps and not go down to the marsh-
    land,—
Muse and recall far off, rather remember than see,—
Lest, on too close sight, I miss the darling illusion,
Spy at their task even here the hands of chance and
    change.

WILFRED CAMPBELL

102.   *Stella Flammarum*

(*An Ode to Halley's Comet*)

STRANGE Wanderer out of the deeps,
   Whence, journeying, come you ?
From what far, unsunned sleeps
   Did fate foredoom you,
Returning for ever again
   Through the surgings of man,
A flaming, awesome portent of dread
   Down the centuries' span ?

WILFRED CAMPBELL

Riddle ! from the dark unwrung
   By all earth's sages ;
God's fiery torch from His hand outflung,
   To flame through the ages :
Thou Satan of planets eterne,
   'Mid angry path,
Chained, in circlings vast, to burn
   Out ancient wrath.

By what dread hand first loosed
   From fires eternal ?
With majesties dire infused
   Of force supernal,
Takest thy headlong way
   O'er the highways of space ?
Oh, wonderful, blossoming flower of fear
   On the sky's far face !

What secrets of destiny's will
   In thy wild burning ?
What portent dire of humanity's ill
   In thy returning ?
Or art thou brand of love
   In masking of bale ?
And bringest thou ever some mystical surcease
   For all who wail ?

Perchance, O Visitor dread,
   Thou hast thine appointed
Task, thou bolt of the vasts outsped !
   With God's anointed,

WILFRED CAMPBELL

Performest some endless toil
   In the universe wide :
Feeding or curing some infinite need
   Where the vast worlds ride.

Once, only once, thy face
   Will I view in this breathing ;
Just for a space thy majesty trace
   'Mid earth's mad seething :
Ere I go hence to my place,
   As thou to thy deeps;
Thou flambent core of a universe dread,
   Where all else sleeps.

But thou and man's spirit are one :
   Thou poet ! Thou flaming
Soul of the dauntless sun,
   Past all reclaiming !
One in that red unrest,
   That yearning, that surge,
That mounting surf of the infinite dream
   O'er eternity's verge.

103.   *Lines on a Skeleton*

THIS was the mightiest house that God e'er made,
   This roofless mansion of the incorruptible.
These joists and bastions once bore walls as fair
As Solomon's palace of white ivory.
Here majesty and love and beauty dwelt,
Shakespeare's wit from these lorn walls looked down.

WILFRED CAMPBELL

Sadness like the autumn made it bare,
Passion like a tempest shook its base,
And joy filled all its halls with ecstasy.

This was the home wherein all dreams of earth
And air and ocean, all supreme delights,
Made mirth and madness : wisdom pored alone ;
And power dominion held : and splendid hope :
And fancy like the delicate sunrise woke
To burgeoning thought and form and melody.

Beneath its dome the agony of the Jew,
The pride of Caesar or the hate of Cain,
The thought of Plato or the heart of Burns,
Once dwelt in some dim form of being's light.

Within these walls of wondrous structure, dread,
A magic lute of elfin melody
Made music immortal, such as never came
From out those ancient halls of Orphean song.

Love dreamed of it, and like a joy it rose.
Power shaped its firm foundations like the base
Of mountain majesty : and o'er its towers
Truth from fair windows made his light look down.

But came a weird and evil demon host,
Besieged its walls, destroyed its marvellous front ;
Shattered its casements, dismantled all its dream,
And hurled it down from out its sunward height ;
And now it lies bereft of all its joy
And pride and power and godlike majesty ;

The sport of elements and hideous mimes,
That blench its corridors, desecrate its rooms,
Where once dwelt love and beauty, joy and hope,
Now tenantless : save for the incurious wind,
And ghostlike rains that beat its bastions bare,
And evil things that creep its chambers through.

But whither thence is fled that tenant rare,
That weird indweller of this wasted house ?
Back from the petalled bloom withdraws the dew,
The melody from the shell, the day from heaven,
To build afar earth's resurrection morn.
And so, Love trusts, in some diviner air
The lord of this lorn mansion dwells in light
Of vaster beauty, vaster scope and dream ;
Where weariness and gladness satiate not,
Where power and splendid being know no ruin,
And evil greeds and envyings work no wrong.

104.   *Wind*

I AM Wind, the deathless dreamer
   Of the summer world ;
Tranced in snows of shade and shimmer,
   On a cloud-scarp curled.

Fluting through the argent shadow
   And the molten shine
Of the golden, lonesome summer
   And its dreams divine.

WILFRED CAMPBELL

All unseen, I walk the meadows,
  Or I wake the wheat,
Speeding o'er the tawny billows
  With my phantom feet.

All the world's face, hushed and sober,
  Wrinkles where I run ;
Turning sunshine into shadow,
  Shadow into sun,

Stirring soft the breast of waters
  With my winnowing wings,
Waking the grey ancient wood
  From hushed imaginings.

Where the blossoms drowse in languors,
  Or a vagrant sips,
Lifting nodding blade or petal
  To my cooling lips ;

Far from gloom of shadowed mountain,
  Surge of sounding sea,
Bud and blossom, leaf and tendril,
  All are glad of me.

Loosed in sunny deeps of heaven,
  Like a dream, I go,
Guiding light my genie-driven
  Flocks, in herds of snow ;—

WILFRED CAMPBELL

Ere I moor them o'er the thirsting
  Woods and fields beneath,
Dumbly yearning, from their burning
  Dream of parchèd death.

Not a sorrow do I borrow
  From the golden day,
Not a shadow holds the meadow
  Where my footsteps stray ;

Light and cool, my kiss is welcome
  Under sun and moon,
To the weary vagrant wending
  Under parchèd noon ;

To the languid, nodding blossom
  In its moonlit dell,
All earth's children, sad and yearning,
  Know and love me well.

Without passion, without sorrow,
  Driven in my dream,
Through the season's trance of sleeping
  Cloud and field and stream,—

Haunting woodlands, lakes and forests,
  Seas and clouds impearled,
I am Wind, the deathless dreamer
  Of the summer world.

105. *The Tragedy of Man*

LONG, long ago ;
　Ere these material days ;
Ere man learned o'er much for the golden glow
　Of Love's divine amaze ;
Ere faith was slain ; there came to this sad earth
　A high, immortal being of source divine,
And mingling with the upward climbing life,
　Like crystal water in some fevered wine,
Wakened in one red blood mysterious strife,
　Knowledge of good and ill, and that sad birth
　Of splendour and woe for all who yearn and pine.

And this is why,
　Down in the craving, remorseful human heart
There doth remain a dream that will not die,
　An unassuagèd hunger, that o'er the smart
Of sorrow and shame and travail, clamours eterne
For some high goal, some vision of being superne,
　Life doth not grant, earth doth not satisfy.

This is the secret of the heart of man
　And his sad tragedy ; his godlike powers ;
His summer of vastness, and the wintry ban
　Of all his greatness high which deity dowers,
Sunk to the yearnings of goat-footed Pan ;
Hinted of Shakespeare and that mighty clan
Of earth's high prophets, who in their brief day,
　Holding the glory of the god in them,

Though chained to cravings of the lesser clay,
　　Dreamed earth's high dreams, and wore love's
　　diadem.

Yea, this is why,
　　Through all earth's travail and joy, her seasons brief
Through all her beauty and genius that will not die,
　　Surges a mighty grief,
Mingling with our heart's best piety;—
　　A sadness, dread, divine,
　　Lifting us beyond the pagan wine
And dance of life,
The satyr clamour and strife,
　　Unto a dream of being, a yearning flame
　　Of that heredity whence our sorrowings came.

106.　　　*The Lyre of Life*

I AM a sad Aeolian lyre,
　　On which the wind of destiny sings
Earth's discords, or her glad desire,
　　Until some dread hand breaks my strings ;—
Until some dread hand makes me mute,
　　And Earth's great organ tones, her roar
　　Of Autumn on his wintry shore;
Old Ocean's voice,
Bidding his mighty hosts rejoice ;
　　Spring's melodies that thrill and soar,
Her viol, oboe, lute, and flute,
　　Reverberate round my heart no more.

WILFRED CAMPBELL

107.   *October Morning*

BRIGHT, pallid, changing, chill October morn :
     Across your windy, keen exhilarant air,
You loom, a cameo dream, a vision fair ;
Where through your purples and mauves of skeleton
     trees,
Friezes of lingering foliage, russet browns,
And wine-like crimsons, flaming torches, gold
Of maples, beeches, sumachs, poplars, shine
The horn-like, cloudy windows of the sky.

Nothing on earth more beautiful than this :
To feel your glow, austere, of wintry flame,
Your exquisite, Greek infinities of colour ;
And know that inward thrill, that Titan vision,
Once more, Atlantean ; the marbled bay,
Th' Olympian mountain, Saturn's mighty crown ;
And hear once more the Tritons sing, and know
Once more, immortal, Earth's old godlike dream.

108.   *The Month of Ripeness*

THOU languid August noon,
     When all the slopes are sunny ;
When with jocund, dreamy tune,
     The bees are in the honey
When with purple flowers,
     A-flaming in the sun,
The drowsy hours
     Thread, one by one,
          The golden pleasaunces.

WILFRED CAMPBELL

Then is heart's musing time,
  Then, of all the seasons,
Old Earth for inward rhyme
  Is full of golden reasons ;—
Then the ripening gourd,
  The sun-kissed garden wall,
The purpling hoard,
  The flocks that call
    Adown the distances.

Forgo the saddening tear,
  Thou Month without alloy ;
To younger seasons of the year
  Resign the flag of joy ;
But thou, be what thou art,
  Full brooding to the brim
Of dreams apart
  And purlieus dim
    Of leafy silences.

109.   *A Canadian Galahad*

(To the memory of Henry Harper, drowned in the Ottawa
River, while trying to save Miss Blair.)

WE crown the splendours of immortal peace,
  And laud the heroes of ensanguined war,
Rearing in granite memory of men
Who build the future, recreate the past,
Or animate the present dull world's pulse
With loftier riches of the human mind.

M 2   163

WILFRED CAMPBELL

But his was greatness not of common mould,
And yet so human in its simple worth,
That any spirit plodding its slow round
Of social commonplace and daily moil,
Might blunder on such greatness, did he hold
In him the kernel sap from which it sprung.

Men in rare hours great actions may perform,
Heroic, lofty, whereof earth will ring,
A world onlooking, and the spirit strung
To high achievement at the cannon's mouth,
Or where fierce ranks of maddened men go down.

But this was godlier. In the common round
Of life's slow action, stumbling on the brink
Of sudden opportunity, he chose
The only noble, godlike, splendid way,
And made his exit, as earth's great have gone,
By that vast doorway looking out on death.

No poet this of winged, immortal pen ;
No hero of a hundred victories ;
Nor iron moulder of unwieldy states,
Grave counsellor of parliaments, gold-tongued,
Standing in shadow of a centuried fame,
Drinking the splendid plaudits of a world.

But simple, unrecorded in his days,
Unostentatious, like the average man
Of average duty, walked the common earth,

And when fate flung her challenge in his face,
Took all his spirit in his blinded eyes,
And showed in action why God made the world.

He passes as all pass, both small and great,
Oblivion-clouded, to the common goal ;—
And all unmindful moves the dull world round,
With baser dreams of this material day,
And all that makes man petty, the slow pace
Of small accomplishment that mocks the soul.

But he hath taught us by this splendid deed
That under all the brutish mask of life,
And dulled intention of ignoble ends,
Man's soul is not all sordid ; that behind
This tragedy of ills and hates that seem
There lurks a godlike impulse in the world,
And men are greater than they idly dream.

110.   *The Mother*

(This poem was suggested by the following passage in Tyler's
Animism : 'The pathetic German superstition that the dead mother's
coming back in the night to suckle the baby she has left on earth
may be known by the hollow pressed down in the bed where
she lay.')

IT was April, blossoming Spring,
They buried me when the birds did sing ;

Earth in clammy wedging earth,
They banked my bed with a black, damp girth.

WILFRED CAMPBELL

Under the damp and under the mould,
I kenned my breasts were clammy and cold.

Out from the red beams, slanting and bright,
I kenned my cheeks were sunken and white.

I was a dream, and the world was a dream,
And yet I kenned all things that seem.

I was a dream, and the world was a dream,
But you cannot bury a red sunbeam.

For though in the under-grave's doom-night
I lay all silent and stark and white,

Yet over my head I seemed to know
The murmurous moods of wind and snow,

The snows that wasted, the winds that blew,
The rays that slanted, the clouds that drew

The water-ghosts up from lakes below,
And the little flower-souls in earth that grow.

Under earth, in the grave's stark night,
I felt the stars and the moon's pale light.

I felt the winds of ocean and land
That whispered the blossoms soft and bland.

Though they had buried me dark and low,
My soul with the season's seemed to grow.

WILFRED CAMPBELL

II

From throes of pain they buried me low,
For death had finished a mother's woe.

But under the sod, in the grave's dread doom,
I dreamed of my baby in glimmer and gloom.

I dreamed of my babe, and I kenned that his rest
Was broken in wailings on my dead breast.

I dreamed that a rose-leaf hand did cling :
Oh, you cannot bury a mother in spring.

When the winds are soft and the blossoms are red
She could not sleep in her cold earth-bed.

I dreamed of my babe for a day and a night,
And then I rose in my grave-clothes white.

I rose like a flower from my damp earth-bed
To the world of sorrowing overhead.

Men would have called me a thing of harm,
But dreams of my babe made me rosy and warm.

I felt my breasts swell under my shroud ;
No stars shone white, no winds were loud ;

But I stole me past the graveyard wall,
For the voice of my baby seemed to call ;

And I kenned me a voice, though my lips were dumb :
Hush, baby, hush ! for mother is come.

WILFRED CAMPBELL

I passed the streets to my husband's home ;
The chamber stairs in a dream I clomb ;

I heard the sound of each sleeper's breath,
Light waves that break on the shores of death.

I listened a space at my chamber door,
Then stole like a moon-ray over its floor.

My babe was asleep on a stranger arm,
' O baby, my baby, the grave is so warm,

' Though dark and so deep, for mother is there !
O come with me from the pain and care !

' O come with me from the anguish of earth,
Where the bed is banked with a blossoming girth,

' Where the pillow is soft and the rest is long,
And mother will croon you a slumber-song,—

' A slumber-song that will charm your eyes
To a sleep that never in earth-song lies !

' The loves of earth your being can spare,
But never the grave, for mother is there.'

I nestled him soft to my throbbing breast,
And stole me back to my long, long rest.

And here I lie with him under the stars,
Dead to earth, its peace and its wars ;

Dead to its hates, its hopes, and its harms,
So long as he cradles up soft in my arms.

And heaven may open its shimmering doors,
And saints make music on pearly floors.

And hell may yawn to its infinite sea,
But they never can take my baby from me.

For so much a part of my soul he hath grown
That God doth know of it high on His throne.

And here I lie with him under the flowers
That sun-winds rock through the billowy hours,

With the night-airs that steal from the murmuring sea,
Bringing sweet peace to my baby and me.

111. *Lines*

On a re-reading of parts of the Old Testament

SUBLIMITY ! Sublimity ! I lay thee down ;
Great Volume of the ages ! older far
Than Cheops' Pyramid or the Parthenon ;
And yet as new as yester-even's star,

That came and burned so bright and pure, across
The world's great weariness and day's decline.
What are all earth's ambitions, gain and loss,
Her hopes ephemeral ; when thou art mine ?

Thou stand'st, a crystal well of water pure,
Amid those fevered fonts of heathen wine,
Graven in truth's deep rock that shall endure,
So greatly human, yet so all divine !

169

This age doth press upon me like a vast,
 Grim adamantine wall of evil doom ;
But when I drink thy living draught, I cast
 Aside this vesture of material gloom ;

These curtains of mortality fall apart ;
 And out, and up, beyond, eternally,
Those stairways of God's ages ; and man's part
 In all that greatness, gone, and yet to be !

112. *The last scene from Mordred*

(The battlefield. Enter ARTHUR *surrounded by knights.)*

ARTHUR. Now where is he, that monster, foul, de-
 formed
 In shape and spirit, nature calls my son ʾ

(Enter MORDRED)

MORDRED. Here !
ARTHUR. Ah, blot on all this sunlight, creature dire,
 Spawn of mine incest ! There standest thou, my sin,
 Incarnate now before me, mine old doom ;
 Thou that wast stronger in thine influences
 To work dread evil in this hideous world
 Than all the glory all my good might win.
MORDRED. Father !
ARTHUR. Yea, well say Father ! Parent I this ill
 That hath enrent my kingdom all in twain.
 In that dread night of my licentious youth,
 When I in darkness thy foul shape begot,

WILFRED CAMPBELL

I worked a web of blackness round my fate
And thine, distorted phantom of my sin,
Not all the tolling of sweet abbey-bells,
And murmur of masses sung these thousand years,
Can sweep from this doomed kingdom.   Father !
  Yea,
There is no truce betwixt us.   Thou art death
To all that I hold dearest on this earth.
Thou stood'st betwixt me and my gladder fate,
The one black spot on all my glory's sun.
In thee once more mine evil blackens in,
Reddens mine eyesight.   Have at thee, foul curse !
MORDRED.   Father !
ARTHUR.   Have at thee !

*(They fight.   ARTHUR wounds MORDRED.   He falls.   A knight
stabs ARTHUR from behind.)*

ARTHUR.   Ho ! all the sunlight blackens !   Mordred !
  Oh !
My glory darkens !   Curtain not yon sun !   *(Dies.)*
MORDRED.   Yea, this is all, and I were made for this,
To scatter death and desolation round
On this fair kingdom, ruin this sweet land,
And level all the pride of Arthur's glory,
As men might level some great castle walls,
And sow with salt the fields of his desire,
And make him mock before the eyes of men ;
Turn all his great joy into bitterness.
Yea, I his blood, and I were made for this.
Oh, ancient, cruel laws of human life,

WILFRED CAMPBELL

Oh, deep, mysterious, unfathomable source
Of man's poor being ; we are ringed about
With such hard rinds of hellish circumstance,
That we can never walk or breathe or hope,
Or eye the sun, or ponder on the green
Of tented plain, or glorious blue of heaven,
Or know love's joy, or knotted thews of strength,
But imps of evil thoughts creep in between,
Like lizards in the chinks of some fair wall,
And mar life's splendour and its greatness all.
'Tis some damned birth-doom blended in the blood,
That prophesies our end in our poor acts.
Oh ! we are but blind children of the dark,
Wending a way we neither make nor ken.
Yea, Arthur, I had loved thee sweet and well,
And made mine arm a bulwark to thy realm,
Had I been but as fair as Lancelot.
What evil germ, false quickening of the blood,
Did breed me foul, distorted as I am,
That I should mar this earth and thy great realm
With my wry, knotted sorrows ? Lancelot's love
Was manly, kind and generous as became
A soul encased in such propitious frame.
The kingly trees well turn them to the sun,
And glory in their splendour with the morn.
'Tis natural that noble souls should dwell
'Twixt noble features ; but the maimèd soul
Should ever be found in the distorted shape.
But I had loved as never man had loved,
Did nature only plant me sweet at first.

(*To his knights.*)   And now I die, and blessed be my
  death,
More blessed far that I had never breathed.
Murder and Treason were my midwives dire,
Rapine and Carnage, priests that shrive me now.

(*Enter* VIVIEN *disguised as a squire.*)

VIVIEN. Mordred, thou diest!
MORDRED. Who art thou?
VIVIEN. I am Vivien.
MORDRED. Hence, hence, Viper, incarnate Fiend!
  Not natural woman, but Ambition framed,
  And all lust's envy.   Thou wert unto me
  A blacker blackness.   Did an angel come
  And whisper sweeter counsel in mine ears,
  And trumpet hopes that all were not in vain ;
  And thou wouldst wool mine ears with malice dire,
  And play upon the black chords of my heart.
  Hence, Devil, hence!   Mar not my closing hours!
VIVIEN. Oh, woe, woe!   (*Steals out.*)
MORDRED. (*To the knights.*)   Now bear me slowly to
  great Arthur's side,
  And let me place my hand upon his breast,
  For he was mine own father!   Alas!   Alas!
  So hideous is this nature we endure!

(*The soldiers place him by Arthur.*)

How calm he sleeps, Allencthon, as those should
Who die in glorious battle.   Dost thou know,
O mighty father, that thine ill-got son,
Ill-got of nature and mysterious night,

WILFRED CAMPBELL

To mar thy splendour and enwreck this world,
Now crawls to thy dead body near his death,
As would some wounded dog of faithful days
To lick his master's hand ? Blame not, O King,
If thou somewhere may know what I here feel,
Thy poor, misshapen Mordred. Blame him not
The turbulent, treacherous currents of the blood
Which were a part of thine ; nor let one thought
Of his past evil mar thy mighty rest.
He would have loved thee ; but remember that.

Now, past is all this splendour ; new worlds come ;
But never more will Britain know such grace,
Such lofty glory, and such splendid days.

Back of the clang of battle, back of all
The mists of life, the clamour and the fall
Of human kingdoms built on human days ;
Arthur ! Merlin ! mighty Dead ! I come !
                              (*Springs to his feet.*)
Ho ! Horse ! To horse ! My sword ! A trumpet
    calls !
A Mordred ! (*Dies.*)

113.   *England*

ENGLAND, England, England,
    Girdled by ocean and skies,
And the power of a world and the heart of a race,
    And a hope that never dies !

England, England, England,
    Wherever a true heart beats,
Wherever the armies of commerce flow,
Wherever the bugles of conquest blow,
Wherever the glories of liberty grow,
    'Tis the name that the world repeats.

And ye, who dwell in the shadow
    Of the century-sculptured piles,
Where sleep our century-honoured dead,
While the great world thunders overhead,
    And far out, miles on miles,
Beyond the throb of the mighty town
    The blue Thames dimples and smiles,—·
Not yours alone the glory of old,
    Of the splendid thousand years
Of Britain's might and Britain's right,
And the brunt of British spears ;—
Not yours alone, for the great world round,
    Ready to dare and do,
Scot and Celt and Norman and Dane,
With the Northman's sinew and heart and brain,
And the Northman's courage for blessing or bane,
    Are England's heroes too.

                              175

WILFRED CAMPBELL

North and South and East and West,
  Wherever their triumphs be,
Their glory goes home to the ocean-girt Isle
Where the heather blooms and the roses smile,
  With the green Isle under her lee.
And if ever the smoke of an alien gun
  Should threaten her iron repose,
Shoulder to shoulder against the world,
  Face to face with her foes,
Scot and Celt and Saxon are one
  Where the glory of England goes.

And we of the newer and vaster West,
  Where the great war-banners are furled,
And commerce hurries her teeming hosts,
And the cannon are silent along our coasts ;
Saxon and Gaul, Canadians claim
A part in the glory and pride and aim
  Of the Empire that girdles the world.

Yea, England, England, England,
  Wherever the daring heart,
By arctic floe or torrid sand
  Thy heroes play their part ;—
For as long as conquest holds the earth,
  Or commerce sweeps the sea,
By orient jungle or western plain
  Will the Saxon spirit be ;

WILFRED CAMPBELL

And whatever the people that dwell beneath
  Or whatever the alien tongue,
Over the freedom and peace of the world
  Is the flag of England flung.

Till the last great freedom is found,
And the last great truth be taught,
Till the last great deed be done,
And the last great battle is fought ;
Till the last great fighter is slain in the last great fight,
And the war-wolf is dead in his den,
England, breeder of hope and valour and might,
Iron mother of men !

Yea, England, England, England,
  Till honour and valour are dead,
Till the world's great cannons rust,
Till the world's great hopes are dust,
  Till faith and freedom be fled ;
Till wisdom and justice have passed
To sleep with those who sleep in the many-chambered
    vast ;—
Till glory and knowledge are charnelled, dust in dust ;
To all that is best in the world's unrest
In heart and mind you are wed ;—
While out from the Indian jungle,
To the far Canadian snows,
Over the east and over the west,
Over the worst and over the best,
The flag of the world to its winds unfurled,
The blood-red ensign blows.

114. *Low Tide on Grand-Prè*

THE sun goes down, and over all
 These barren reaches by the tide
Such unelusive glories fall,
  I almost dream they yet will bide
  Until the coming of the tide.

.And yet I know that not for us,
  By any ecstasy of dream,
He lingers to keep luminous
  A little while the grievous stream,
  Which frets, uncomforted of dream ;—

A grievous stream, that to and fro,
  All through the fields of Acadie
Goes wandering, as if to know
  Why one belovèd face should be
  So long from home and Acadie !

Was it a year or lives ago
  We took the grasses on our hands,
And caught the summer flying low
  Over the waving meadow-lands,
  And held it there between our hands ?

The while the river at our feet—
  A drowsy inland meadow stream—
At set of sun the after-heat
  Made running gold, and in the gleam
  We freed our birch upon the stream.

178

BLISS CARMAN

There down along the elms at dusk
  We lifted dripping blade to drift,
Through twilight scented fine like musk
  Where night and gloom awhile uplift,
  Nor sunder soul and soul adrift.

And that we took into our hands—
  Spirit of life or subtler thing—
Breathed on us there, and loosed the bands
  Of death, and taught us, whispering,
  The secret of some wonder-thing.

Then all your face grew light, and seemed
  To hold the shadow of the sun ;
The evening faltered, and I deemed
  That time was ripe, and years had done.
  Their wheeling underneath the sun.

So all desire and all regret,
  And fear and memory, were naught ;
One to remember or forget
  The keen delight our hearts had caught ;
  Morrow and yesterday were naught !

The night has fallen, and the tide. . . .
  Now and again comes drifting home,
Across these aching barrens wide,
  A sigh like driven wind or foam ;
  In grief the flood is bursting home !

BLISS CARMAN

Spring Song

MAKE me over, mother April,
    When the sap begins to stir !
When thy flowery hand delivers
All the mountain-prisoned rivers,
And thy great heart beats and quivers
To revive the days that were,
Make me over, mother April,
When the sap begins to stir !

Take my dust and all my dreaming,
Count my heart-beats one by one,
Send them where the winters perish ;
Then some golden noon recherish
And restore them in the sun,
Flower and scent and dust and dreaming,
With their heart-beats every one !

Set me in the urge and tide-drift
Of the streaming hosts a-wing !
Breast of scarlet, throat of yellow,
Raucous challenge, wooings mellow—
Every migrant is my fellow,
Making northward with the spring.
Loose me in the urge and tide-drift
Of the streaming hosts a-wing !

Shrilling pipe or fluting whistle,
In the valleys come again ;
Fife of frog and call of tree-toad,

BLISS CARMAN

All my brothers, five or three-toed,
With their revel no more vetoed,
Making music in the rain ;
Shrilling pipe or fluting whistle,
In the valleys come again.

Make me of thy seed to-morrow,
When the sap begins to stir !
Tawny light-foot, sleepy bruin,
Bright-eyes in the orchard ruin,
Gnarl the good life goes askew in,
Whisky-jack, or tanager,—
Make me anything to-morrow,
When the sap begins to stir !

Make me even (how do I know ?)
Like my friend the gargoyle there ;
It may be the heart within him
Swells that doltish hands should pin him
Fixed for ever in mid-air.
Make me even sport for swallows,
Like the soaring gargoyle there !

Give me the old clue to follow
Through the labyrinth of night !
Clod of clay with heart of fire,
Things that burrow and aspire,
With the vanishing desire
For the perishing delight,—
Only the old clue to follow
Through the labyrinth of night !

BLISS CARMAN

Make me over, mother April,
When the sap begins to stir !
Fashion me from swamp or meadow,
Garden plot or ferny shadow,
Hyacinth or humble bur !
Make me over, mother April,
When the sap begins to stir !

Let me hear the far low summons
When the silver winds return ;
Rills that run and streams that stammer,
Golden wing with his loud hammer,
Icy brooks that brawl and clamour
Where the Indian willows burn ;
Let me hearken to the calling
When the silver winds return,

Till recurring and recurring,
Long since wandered and come back,
Like a whim of Grieg's or Gounod's,
This same self, bird, bud, or bluenose,
Some day I may capture, (who knows ?)
Just the one last joy I lack,
Waking to the far new summons,
When the old spring winds come back.

For I have no choice of being,
When the sap begins to climb,—
Strong insistence, sweet intrusion,
Vasts and verges of illusion,—

BLISS CARMAN

So I win to time's confusion,
The one perfect pearl of time,
Joy and joy and joy for ever,
Till the sap forgets to climb!

Make me over in the morning
From the rag-bag of the world!
Scraps of dream and duds of daring,
Home-brought stuff from far sea-faring,
Faded colours once so flaring,
Shreds of banners long since furled!
Hues of ash and glints of glory,
In the rag-bag of the world!

Let me taste the old immortal
Indolence of life once more;
Not recalling nor foreseeing,
Let the great slow joys of being
Well my heart through as of yore!
Let me taste the old immortal
Indolence of life once more!

Give me the old drink for rapture,
The delirium to drain,
All my fellows drank in plenty
At the Three Score Inns and Twenty
From the mountains to the main!
Give me the old drink for rapture,
The delirium to drain!

BLISS CARMAN

Only make me over, April,
When the sap begins to stir !
Make me man or make me woman,
Make me oaf or ape or human,
Cup of flower or cone of fir;
Make me anything but neuter
When the sap begins to stir !

116.   *Hack and Hew*

HACK and Hew were the sons of God
    In the earlier earth than now ;
One at his right hand, one at his left,
    To obey as he taught them how.

And Hack was blind, and Hew was dumb,
    But both had the wild, wild heart ;
And God's calm will was their burning will,
    And the gist of their toil was art.

They made the moon and the belted stars,
    They set the sun to ride ;
They loosed the girdle and veil of the sea,
    The wind and the purple tide.

Both flower and beast beneath their hands
    To beauty and speed out-grew,—
The furious, fumbling hand of Hack,
    And the glorying hand of Hew.
184

BLISS CARMAN

Then, fire and clay, they fashioned a man,
  And painted him rosy brown ;
And God himself blew hard in his eyes ;
  ' Let them burn till they smoulder down ! '

And ' There ! ' said Hack, and ' There ! ' thought Hew,
  ' We'll rest, for our toil is done.'
But ' Nay ', the Master Workman said,
  ' For your toil is just begun.

' And ye who served me of old as God,
  Shall serve me anew as man,
Till I compass the dream that is my heart,
  And perfect the vaster plan.'

And still the craftsman over his craft,
  In the vague white light of dawn,
With God's calm will for his burning will,
  While the mounting day comes on,

Yearning, wind-swift, indolent, wild,
  Toils with those shadowy two,—
The faltering, restless hand of Hack,
  And the tireless hand of Hew.

BLISS CARMAN

The Gravedigger

OH ! the shambling sea is a sexton old,
  And well his work is done,
With an equal grave for lord and knave,
  He buries them every one.

   Then hoy and rip, with a rolling hip,
     He makes for the nearest shore ;
   And God, who sent him a thousand ship,
     Will send him a thousand more ;
   But some he'll save for a bleaching grave,
     And shoulder them in to shore—
   Shoulder them in, shoulder them in,
     Shoulder them in to shore.

   Oh ! the ships of Greece and the ships of Tyre
     Went out, and where are they ?
   In the port they made, they are delayed
     With the ships of yesterday.

   He followed the ships of England far,
     As the ships of long ago ;
   And the ships of France they led him a dance,
     But he laid them all arow.

   Oh, a loafing, idle lubber to him
     Is the sexton of the town ;
   For sure and swift, with a guiding lift,
     He shovels the dead men down.
   186

BLISS CARMAN

But though he delves so fierce and grim,
 His honest graves are wide,
As well they know who sleep below
 The dredge of the deepest tide.

Oh, he works with a rollicking stave at lip,
 And loud is the chorus skirled ;
With the burly rote of his rumbling throat
 He batters it down the world.

He learned it once in his father's house,
 Where the ballads of eld were sung ;
And merry enough is the burden rough,
 But no man knows the tongue.

Oh ! fair, they say, was his bride to see,
 And wilful she must have been,
That she could bide at his gruesome side
 When the first red dawn came in.

And sweet, they say, is her kiss to those
 She greets to his border home ;
And softer than sleep her hand's first sweep
 That beckons, and they come.

Oh ! crooked is he, but strong enough
 To handle the tallest mast ;
From the royal barque to the slaver dark,
 He buries them all at last.

Then hoy and rip, with a rolling hip,
   He makes for the nearest shore ;
And God, who sent him a thousand ship,
   Will send him a thousand more ;
But some he'll save for a bleaching grave,
   And shoulder them in to shore—
Shoulder them in, shoulder them in,
   Shoulder them in to shore.

118.   *Songs of the Sea Children*

•VI

' Love, by that loosened hair '

LOVE, by that loosened hair,
   Well now I know
Where the lost Lilith went
   So long ago.

Love, by those starry eyes
   I understand
How the seamaidens lure
   Mortals from land.

Love, by that welling laugh
   Joy claims its own
Sea-born and wind-wayward
   Child of the sun.

BLISS CARMAN

119.   '*Let the red dawn surmise*'

LET the red dawn surmise
   What we shall do,
When this blue starlight dies
   And all is through.

· If we have loved but well
   Under the sun,
Let the last morrow tell
   What we have done.

120.   '*I was a reed in the stilly stream*'

I WAS a reed in the stilly stream,
   Heigh-ho !
And thou my fellow of moveless dream,
   Heigh-ho !

Hardly a word the river said
As there we bowed him a listless head :

Only the yellowbird pierced the noon :
And summer died to a drowsier swoon,

Till the little wind of night came by,
With the little stars in the lonely sky,

And the little leaves that only stir,
When the shyest wood-fellows confer.

It shook the stars in their purple sphere,
And laid a frost on the lips of fear.

It woke our slumbering desire
As a breath that blows a mellow fire,

And the thrill that made the forest start
Was a little sigh from our happy heart.

This is the story of the world,
   Heigh-ho !
This is the glory of the world,
   Heigh-ho !

LIII

121.   *' I think the sun when he turns at night '*

I THINK the sun when he turns at night,
   And lays his face against the seas,
Must have such thoughts as these.

I think the wind, when he wakes at dawn,
Must wonder, seeing hill by hill,
That they can sleep so still.

122.   *A Son of the Sea*

I WAS born for deep-sea faring ;
   I was bred to put to sea ;
Stories of my father's daring
   Filled me at my mother's knee.

I was sired among the surges ;
   I was cubbed beside the foam ;
All my heart is in its verges,
   And the sea wind is my home.

All my boyhood, from far vernal
  Bourns of being, came to me,
Dream-like, plangent, and eternal
  Memories of the plunging sea.

123.   *Overlord*

LORD of the grass and hill,
    Lord of the rain,
White overlord of will,
    Master of pain.

I, who am dust and air,
    Blown through the halls of death
Like a pale ghost of prayer,
    I am thy breath.

Lord of the blade and leaf,
    Lord of the bloom,
Sheer overlord of grief,
    Master of doom,

Lonely as wind or snow,
    Through the vague world and dim,
Vagrant and glad I go,
    I am thy whim.

Lord of the storm and lull,
    Lord of the sea,
I am thy broken gull
    Blown out alee.

BLISS CARMAN

Lord of the harvest dew,
  Lord of the dawn,
Star of the paling blue
  Darkling and gone,

Lost on the mountain height
  Where the first winds are stirred,
Out of the wells of night,
  I am thy word.

Lord of the haunted hush
  Where raptures throng,
I am thy hermit thrush
  Ending no song.

Lord of the frost and cold,
  Lord of the north,
When the red sun grows old
  And day goes forth,

I shall put off this girth—
  Go glad and free,
Earth to my mother earth,
  Spirit to thee.

124.   *The Players*

WE are the players of a play
  As old as earth,
Between the wings of night and day,
  With tears and mirth.

BLISS CARMAN

There is no record of the land
   From whence it came,
No legend of the playwright's hand,
   No bruited fame

Of those who for the piece were cast
   On that first night,
When God drew up His curtain vast :
   And there was light.

·Before our eyes as we come on,
   From age to age,
Flare up the footlights of the dawn
   On this round stage.

In front, unknown, beyond the glare
   Vague shadows loom ;
And sounds like muttering winds are there
   Foreboding doom.

Yet wistfully we keep the boards ;
   And as we mend
The blundering forgotten words,
   Hope to the end

To hear the storm-beat of applause
   Fill our desire
When the dark prompter gives us pause,
   And we retire.

125.   *In the Heart of the Hills*

IN the warm blue heart of the hills
    My beautiful beautiful one
Sleeps where he laid him down
    Before the journey was done.

All the long summer day
    The ghosts of noon draw nigh,
And the tremulous aspens hear
    The footing of winds go by.

Down to the gates of the sea,
    Out of the gates of the west,
Journeys the whispering river
    Before the place of his rest.

The road he loved to follow
    When June came by his door,
Out through the dim blue haze
    Leads, but allures no more.

The trailing shadows of clouds
    Steal from the slopes and are gone :
The myriad life in the grass
    Stirs, but he slumbers on ;

The inland-wandering tern
    Skriel as they forage and fly ;
His loons on the lonely reach
    Utter their querulous cry ;

194

BLISS CARMAN

Over the floating lilies
   A dragon-fly tacks and steers ;
Far in the depth of the blue
   A martin settles and veers ;

To every roadside thistle
   A gold-brown butterfly clings ;
But he no more companions
   All the dear vagrant things.

The strong red journeying sun,
   The pale and wandering rain,
Will roam on the hills together
   And find him never again.

Then twilight falls with the touch
   Of a hand that soothes and stills,
And a swamp-robin sings into light
   The lone white star of the hills.

Alone in the dusk he sings,
   And a burden of sorrow and wrong
Is lifted up from the earth
   And carried away in his song.

Alone in the dusk he sings,
   And the joy of another day
Is folded in peace and borne
   On the drift of years away.

But there in the heart of the hills
   My beautiful weary one
Sleeps where I laid him down ;
   And the long sweet night is begun.

126.   *Sappho Lyrics*

XXIII

' I loved thee, Atthis, in the long ago

I LOVED thee, Atthis, in the long ago,
    When the great oleanders were in flower
In the broad herded meadows full of sun.
And we would often at the fall of dusk
Wander together by the silver stream,
When the soft grass-heads were all wet with dew
And purple-misted in the fading light.
And joy I knew and sorrow at thy voice,
And the superb magnificence of love,—
The loneliness that saddens solitude,
And the sweet speech that makes it durable,—
The bitter longing and the keen desire,
The sweet companionship of quiet days
In the slow ample beauty of the world,
And the unutterable glad release
Within the temple of the holy night.
O Atthis, how I loved thee long ago
In that fair perished summer by the sea !

LX

127.   *' When I have departed '*

WHEN I have departed
    Say but this behind me,
' Love·was all her wisdom,
    All her care.

BLISS CARMAN

' Well she kept Love's secret,—
Dared and never faltered,—
Laughed and never doubted
    Love would win.

' Let the world's rough triumph
Trample by above her,
She is safe for ever
    From all harm.

' In a land that knows not
Bitterness nor sorrow,
She has found out all
    Of truth at last.'

ARCHIBALD LAMPMAN

128.   *Among the Millet*

THE dew is gleaming in the grass,
  The morning hours are seven,
And I am fain to watch you pass,
  Ye soft white clouds of heaven.

Ye stray and gather, part and fold ;
  The wind alone can tame you ;
I think of what in time of old
  The poets loved to name you.

They called you sheep, the sky your sward,
   A field without a reaper ;
They called the shining sun your lord,
   The shepherd wind your keeper.

Your sweetest poets I will deem
   The men of old for moulding
In simple beauty such a dream,
   And I could lie beholding,

Where daisies in the meadow toss,
   The wind from morn till even
For ever shepherd you across
   The shining field of heaven.

129.   *Heat*

FROM plains that reel to southward, dim,
   The road runs by me white and bare ;
Up the steep hill it seems to swim
   Beyond, and melt into the glare.

Upward half-way, or it may be
   Nearer the summit, slowly steals
A hay-cart, moving dustily
   With idly clacking wheels.

By his cart's side the wagoner
   Is slouching slowly at his ease,
Half hidden in the windless blur
   Of white dust puffing to his knees.

198

ARCHIBALD LAMPMAN

This wagon on the height above,
  From sky to sky, on either hand,
Is the sole thing that seems to move
  In all the heat-held land.

Beyond me in the fields the sun
  Soaks in the grass and hath his will ;
I count the marguerites one by one ;
  Even the buttercups are still.

On the brook yonder not a breath
  Disturbs the spider or the midge ;
The water-bugs draw close beneath
  The cool gloom of the bridge.

Where the far elm-tree shadows flood
  Dark patches in the burning grass,
The cows, each with her peaceful cud,
  Lie waiting for the heat to pass.

From somewhere on the slope near by,
  Into the pale depth of the noon
A wandering thrush slides leisurely
  His thin revolving tune.

In intervals of dreams I hear
  The cricket from the droughty ground ;
The grasshoppers spin into mine ear
  A small innumerable sound.

I lift mine eyes sometimes to gaze ;
  The burning sky-line blinds my sight ;
The woods far-off are blue with haze ;
  The hills are drenched in light.

And yet to me not this or that
  Is always sharp or always sweet ;
In the sloped shadow of my hat
  I lean at rest, and drain the heat ;

Nay more, I think some blessèd power
  Hath brought me wandering idly here ;
In the full furnace of this hour
  My thoughts grow keen and clear.

130.   *The Frogs*

I

BREATHERS of wisdom won without a quest,
  Quaint uncouth dreamers, voices high and strange ;
  Flutists of lands where beauty hath no change,
And wintry grief is a forgotten guest ;
Sweet murmurers of everlasting rest,
  For whom glad days have ever yet to run,
  And moments are as aeons, and the sun
But ever sunken half-way toward the west.

Often to me who heard you in your day,
  With close wrapt ears, it could not choose but seem
That earth, our mother, searching in what way
  Men's hearts might know her spirit's inmost dream,
Ever at rest beneath life's change and stir,
Made you her soul, and bade you pipe for her.

200

ARCHIBALD LAMPMAN

II

In those mute days when spring was in her glee,
  And hope was strong, we knew not why or how,
  And earth, the mother, dreamed with brooding brow,
Musing on life, and what the hours might be,
When love should ripen to maternity,
    Then like high flutes in silvery interchange
    Ye piped with voices still and sweet and strange,
And ever as ye piped, on every tree

The great buds swelled ; among the pensive woods
    The spirits of first flowers awoke and flung
From buried faces the close-fitting hoods,
    And listened to your piping till they fell,
    The frail spring-beauty with her perfumed bell,
      The wind-flower, and the spotted adder-tongue.

III

All the day long, wherever pools might be
  Among the golden meadows, where the air
  Stood in a dream, as it were moored there
For ever in a noontide reverie,
Or where the birds made riot of their glee
    In the still woods, and the hot sun shone down,
    Crossed with warm lucent shadows on the brown
Leaf-paven pools, that bubbled dreamily.

Or far away in whispering river meads
  And watery marshes where the brooding noon,
  Full with the wonder of its own sweet boon,
Nestled and slept among the noiseless reeds,
    Yet sat and murmured, motionless as they,
    With eyes that dreamed beyond the night and day

ARCHIBALD LAMPMAN

IV

And when day passed and over Heaven's height,
  Thin with the many stars and cool with dew,
  The fingers of the hours slowly drew
The wonder of the ever healing night,
No grief or loneliness or rapt delight
  Or weight of silence ever brought to you
  Slumber or rest ; only your voices grew
More high and solemn ; slowly with hushed flight

Ye saw the echoing hours go by, long-drawn,
  Nor ever stirred, watching with fathomless eyes,
  And with your countless clear antiphonies
Filling the earth and heaven, even till dawn,
  Last-risen, found you with its first pale gleam,
  Still with soft throats unaltered in your dream.

V

And slowly as we heard you, day by day,
  The stillness of enchanted reveries
  Bound brain and spirit and half-closèd eyes,
In some divine sweet wonder-dream astray ;
To us no sorrow or upreared dismay
  Nor any discord came, but evermore
  The voices of mankind, the outer roar,
Grew strange and murmurous, faint and far away

Morning and noon and midnight exquisitely,
  Rapt with your voices, this alone we knew,
Cities might change and fall, and men might die,
  Secure were we, content to dream with you
That change and pain are shadows faint and fleet,
And dreams are real, and life is only sweet.

131. *Knowledge*

WHAT is more large than knowledge, and more
    sweet ;
  Knowledge of thoughts and deeds, of rights and
    wrongs,
  Of passions, and of beauties, and of songs ;
Knowledge of life ; to feel its great heart beat .
Through all the soul upon her crystal seat ;
  To see, to feel, and evermore to know ;
  To till the old world's wisdom till it grow
A garden for the wandering of our feet.

Oh for a life of leisure and broad hours,
  To think and dream, to put away small things,
    This world's perpetual leaguer of dull noughts ;
To wander like the bee among the flowers
  Till old age find us weary, feet and wings
    Grown heavy with the gold of many thoughts.

132. *A Prayer*

O EARTH, O dewy mother, breathe on us
  Something of all thy beauty and thy might,
Us that are part of day, but most of night,
Not strong like thee, but ever burdened thus
With glooms and cares, things pale and dolorous,
  Whose gladdest moments are not wholly bright ;
  Something of all thy freshness and thy light,
O earth, O mighty mother, breathe on us.

O mother, who wast long before our day,
  And after us full many an age shalt be,
Careworn and blind, we wander from thy way :
  Born of thy strength, yet weak and halt are we :
Grant us, O mother, therefore, us who pray,
Some little of thy light and majesty.

133.   *The Truth*

FRIEND, though thy soul should burn thee, yet be
    still.
  Thoughts were not made for strife, nor tongues for
    swords.
  He that sees clear is gentlest of his words,
And that 's not truth that hath the heart to kill.
The whole world's thought shall not one truth fulfil.
  Dull in our age, and passionate in youth,
  No mind of man hath found the perfect truth,
Nor shalt thou find it ; therefore, friend, be still.

Watch and be still, nor hearken to the fool,
The babbler of consistency and rule :
Wisest is he, who, never quite secure,
  Changes his thoughts for better day by day.
To-morrow some new light will shine, be sure,
  And thou shalt see thy thought another way.

134.   *Midsummer Night*

MOTHER of balms and soothings manifold,
      Quiet-breathed Night, whose brooding hours
         are seven,
   To whom the voices of all rest are given,
And those few stars whose scattered names are told.
Far off, beyond the westward hills outrolled,
   Darker than thou, more still, more dreamy even,
   The golden moon leans in the dusky heaven,
And under her, one star, a point of gold.

And all go slowly lingering toward the west,
As we go down forgetfully to our rest,
   Weary of daytime, tired of noise and light.
Ah, it was time that thou shouldst come, for we
Were sore athirst, and had great need of thee,
   Thou sweet physician, balmy-bosomed Night.

135.   *The Larger Life*

I

I LIE upon my bed and hear and see.
   The moon is rising through the glistening trees ;
And momently a great and sombre breeze,
With a vast voice returning fitfully,
Comes like a deep-toned grief, and stirs in me,
Somehow, by some inexplicable art,
A sense of my soul's strangeness, and its part
In the dark march of human destiny.

What am I then, and what are they that pass
Yonder, and love and laugh, and mourn and weep ?
What shall they know of me, or I, alas !
Of them ? Little. At times, as if from sleep,
We waken to this yearning passionate mood,
And tremble at our spiritual solitude.

II

Nay, never once to feel we are alone,
While the great human heart around us lies :
To make the smile on other lips our own,
To live upon the light in other eyes :
To breathe without a doubt the limpid air
Of that most perfect love that knows no pain :
To say ' I love you ' only, and not care
Whether the love come back to us again,
Divinest self-forgetfulness, at first
A task, and then a tonic, then a need ;
To greet with open hands the best and worst,
And only for another's wounds to bleed :
This is to see the beauty that God meant,
Wrapped round with life, ineffably content.

III

There is a beauty at the goal of life,
A beauty growing since the world began,
Through every age and race, through lapse and strife
Till the great human soul complete her span.

Beneath the waves of storm that lash and burn,
The currents of blind passion that appal,
To listen and keep watch till we discern
The tide of sovereign truth that guides it all :
So to address our spirits to the height,
And so attune them to the valiant whole,
That the great light be clearer for our light,
And the great soul the stronger for our soul :
To have done this is to have lived, though fame
Remember us with no familiar name.

136.   *September*

NOW hath the summer reached her golden close,
    And lost, amid her cornfields, bright of soul,
Scarcely perceives from her divine repose
    How near, how swift, the inevitable goal :
Still, still, she smiles, though from her careless feet
    The bounty and the fruitful strength are gone,
    And through the soft long wondering days goes on
The silent sere decadence sad and sweet.

The kingbird and the pensive thrush are fled,
    Children of light, too fearful of the gloom ;
The sun falls low, the secret word is said,
    The mouldering woods grow silent as the tomb ;
Even the fields have lost their sovereign grace,
    The cone-flower and the marguerite ; and no more,
    Across the river's shadow-haunted floor,
The paths of skimming swallows interlace.

ARCHIBALD LAMPMAN

Already in the outland wilderness
   The forests echo with unwonted dins ;
In clamorous gangs the gathering woodmen press
   Northward, and the stern winter's toil begins.
Around the long low shanties, whose rough lines
   Break the sealed dreams of many an unnamed lake,
   Already in the frost-clear morns awake
The crash and thunder of the falling pines.

Where the tilled earth, with all its fields set free,
   Naked and yellow from the harvest lies,
By many a loft and busy granary,
   The hum and tumult of the threshers rise ;
There the tanned farmers labour without slack,
   Till twilight deepens round the spouting mill,
   Feeding the loosened sheaves, or with fierce will,
Pitching waist deep upon the dusty stack.

Still a brief while, ere the old year quite pass,
   Our wandering steps and wistful eyes shall greet
The leaf, the water, the belovèd grass ;
   Still from these haunts and this accustomed seat
I see the wood-wrapt city, swept with light,
   The blue long-shadowed distance, and, between,
   The dotted farm-lands with their parcelled green,
The dark pine forest and the watchful height.

I see the broad rough meadow stretched away
   Into the crystal sunshine, wastes of sod,
Acres of withered vervain, purple-grey,
   Branches of aster, groves of golden-rod ;

ARCHIBALD LAMPMAN

And yonder, towards the sunlit summit, strewn
   With shadowy boulders, crowned and swathed with
      weed,
   Stand ranks of silken thistles, blown to seed,
Long silver fleeces shining like the noon.

In far-off russet cornfields, where the dry
   Grey shocks stand peaked and withering, half con-
      cealed
In the rough earth, the orange pumpkins lie,
   Full-ribbed ; and in the windless pasture-field
The sleek red horses o'er the sun-warmed ground
   Stand pensively about in companies,
   While all around them from the motionless trees
The long clean shadows sleep without a sound.

Under cool elm-trees floats the distant stream,
   Moveless as air ; and o'er the vast warm earth
The fathomless daylight seems to stand and dream,
   A liquid cool elixir—all its girth
Bound with faint haze, a frail transparency,
   Whose lucid purple barely veils and fills
   The utmost valleys and the thin last hills,
Nor mars one whit their perfect clarity.

Thus without grief the golden days go by,
   So soft we scarcely notice how they wend,
And like a smile half happy, or a sigh,
   The summer passes to her quiet end ;

And soon, too soon, around the cumbered eaves
 Sly frosts shall take the creepers by surprise,
 And through the wind-touched reddening woods
  shall rise
October with the rain of ruined leaves.

137.   *Snowbirds*

ALONG the narrow sandy height
 I watch them swiftly come and go,
  Or round the leafless wood,
  Like flurries of wind-driven snow,
 Revolving in perpetual flight,
  A changing multitude.

Nearer and nearer still they sway,
 And, scattering in a circled sweep,
  Rush down without a sound ;
  And now I see them peer and peep,
 Across yon level bleak and grey,
  Searching the frozen ground—

Until a little wind upheaves
 And makes a sudden rustling there,
  And then they drop their play,
  Flash up into the sunless air,
 And, like a flight of silver leaves,
  Swirl round and sweep away.

FREDERICK G. SCOTT

138.   *The King's Bastion*

FIERCE on this bastion beats the noonday sun ;
  The city sleeps beneath me, old and grey ;
On convent roofs the quivering sunbeams play,
And batteries guarded by dismantled gun.
No breeze comes from the northern hills that run
  Circling the blue mist of the summer's day ;
No ripple stirs the great stream on its way
To those dim headlands where its rest is won.

Ah God, what thunders shook these crags of yore,
  What smoke of battle rolled about this place,
    What strife of worlds in pregnant agony !
Now all is hushed, yet here, in dreams, once more
  We catch the echoes, ringing back from space,
    Of God's strokes forging human history.

139.   *In Memoriam*

GROWING to full manhood now,
  With the care-lines on our brow,
We, the youngest of the nations,
With no childish lamentations,
Weep, as only strong men weep,
For the noble hearts that sleep,
Pillowed where they fought and bled,
The loved and lost, our glorious dead !

FREDERICK G. SCOTT

Toil and sorrow come with age,
Manhood's rightful heritage ;
Toil our arms more strong shall render
Sorrow make our heart more tender,
In the heartlessness of time ;
Honour lays a wreath sublime—
Deathless glory—where they bled,
Our loved and lost, our glorious dead !

Wild the prairie grasses wave
O'er each hero's new-made grave ;
Time shall write such wrinkles o'er us,
But the future spreads before us
Glorious in that sunset land—
Nerving every heart and hand,
Comes a brightness none can shed,
But the dead, the glorious dead !

Lay them where they fought and fell ;
Every heart shall ring their knell,
For the lessons they have taught us,
For the glory they have brought us.
Though our hearts are sad and bowed,
Nobleness still makes us proud—
Proud of light their names shall shed
In the roll-call of our dead !

Growing to full manhood now,
With the care-lines on our brow,
We, the youngest of the nations,
With no childish lamentations,

Weep, as only strong men weep,
For the noble hearts that sleep,
Where the call of duty led,
Where the lonely prairies spread,
Where for us they fought and bled,
Our ever loved and glorious dead !

140.   *Van Elsen*

GOD spake three times and saved Van Elsen's soul ;
He spake by sickness first and made him whole ;
    Van Elsen heard Him not,
    Or soon forgot.

God spake to him by wealth ; the world outpoured
Its treasures at his feet, and called him Lord ;
    Van Elsen's heart grew fat
    And proud thereat.

God spake the third time when the great world smiled,
And in the sunshine slew his little child ;
    Van Elsen like a tree
    Fell hopelessly.

Then in the darkness came a voice which said,
' As thy heart bleedeth, so my heart hath bled,
    As I have need of thee,
    Thou needest me.'

That night Van Elsen kissed the baby feet,
And kneeling by the narrow winding sheet,
    Praised Him with fervent breath
    Who conquered death.

FREDERICK G. SCOTT

141.   *The Unnamed Lake*

IT sleeps among the thousand hills
  Where no man ever trod,
And only nature's music fills
  The silences of God.

Great mountains tower above its shore,
  Green rushes fringe its brim,
And o'er its breast for evermore
  The wanton breezes skim.

Dark clouds that intercept the sun
  Go there in Spring to weep.
And there, when Autumn days are done,
  White mists lie down to sleep.

Sunrise and sunset crown with gold
  The peaks of ageless stone,
Where winds have thundered from of old
  And storms have set their throne.

No echoes of the world afar
  Disturb it night or day,
But sun and shadow, moon and star,
  Pass and repass for ay.

'Twas in the grey of early dawn
  When first the lake we spied,
And fragments of a cloud were drawn
  Half down the mountain side.

FREDERICK G. SCOTT

Along the shore a heron flew,
  And from a speck on high,
That hovered in the deepening blue,
  We heard the fish-hawk's cry.

Among the cloud-capt solitudes
  No sound the silence broke,
Save when, in whispers down the woods,
  The guardian mountains spoke.

Through tangled brush and dewy brake,
  Returning whence we came,
We passed in silence, and the lake
  We left without a name.

142. *The Heaven of Love*

I ROSE at midnight and beheld the sky
  Sown thick with stars, like grains of golden sand
  Which God had scattered loosely from His hand
Upon the floorways of His house on high ;
And straight I pictured to my spirit's eye
  The giant worlds, their course by wisdom planned,
  The weary wastes, the gulfs no sight hath spanned,
And endless time for ever passing by.

Then, filled with wonder and a secret dread,
  I crept to where my child lay fast asleep,
With chubby arm beneath his golden head.
  What cared I then for all the stars above ?
  One little face shut out the boundless deep,
    One little heart revealed the heaven of love.

FREDERICK G. SCOTT

143. *Easter Island*

THERE lies a lone isle in the tropic seas,—
A mountain isle, with beaches shining white,
  Where soft stars smile upon its sleep by night,
And every noonday fans it with a breeze.
Here on a cliff, carved upward from the knees,
  Three uncouth statues of gigantic height,
  Upon whose brows the circling sea-birds light,
Stare out to ocean over the tall trees.

For ever gaze they at the sea and sky,
  For ever hear the thunder of the main,
    For ever watch the ages die away;
And ever round them rings the phantom cry
  Of some lost race that died in human pain,
    Looking toward heaven, yet seeing no more than
      they.

144. *In the Woods*

THIS is God's house—the blue sky is the ceiling,
  This wood the soft green carpet for His feet,
Those hills His stairs, down which the brooks come
      stealing
  With baby laughter, making earth more sweet.

And here His friends come, clouds, and soft winds
      sighing,
  And little birds whose throats pour forth their love,
And spring and summer, and the white snow lying
  Pencilled with shadows of bare boughs above.

216

FREDERICK G. SCOTT

And here come sunbeams through the green leaves
    straying,
  And shadows from the storm-clouds over-drawn,
And warm, hushed nights, when Mother Earth is
    praying
  So late that her moon-candle burns till dawn.

Sweet house of God, sweet earth, so full of pleasure,
  I enter at thy gates in storm or calm ;
And every sunbeam is a joy or pleasure,
  And every cloud a solace and a balm.

145.　　　　　*The River*

WHY hurry, little river ?
    Why hurry to the sea ?
There is nothing there to do
But to sink into the blue
    And all forgotten be.
There is nothing on that shore
But the tides for evermore,
And the faint and far-off line
Where the winds across the brine
For ever, ever roam
And never find a home.

Why hurry, little river,
  From the mountains and the mead,
Where the graceful elms are sleeping
  And the quiet cattle feed ?

The loving shadows cool
The deep and restful pool,
And every tribute stream
Brings its own sweet woodland dream
Of the mighty woods that sleep
Where the sighs of earth are deep,
And the silent skies look down
On the savage mountain's frown.

Oh, linger, little river !
   Your banks are all so fair,
Each morning is a hymn of praise,
   Each evening is a prayer.
All day the sunbeams glitter
   On your shallows and your bars,
And at night the dear God stills you
   With the music of the stars.

146.   *The Temple of the Ages*

THESE mountains sleep, with winter's mantle
   round them,
  The thunder's voice no longer breaks their rest ;
From bluest heights the sun beholds with rapture
  The noble pose of each gigantic crest.

The generations of the clouds have vanished
  Which lingered idly here through autumn days ;
The leaves have gone, the voices of the tempest
  No longer roll to heaven their hymn of praise.
   218

FREDERICK G. SCOTT

Deep hid in snow, the streams with muffled murmurs
   Pour down dark caverns to the infinite sea ;
This awful peace has vexed their restless childhood ;
   They hurry from its dread solemnity.

Even the climbing woods are mute and spellbound,
   And halting midway on the steep ascent,
The patient spruces hold their breath for wonder,
   Nor shake the snow with which their boughs are
      bent.

Now as the sun goes down with all his shining,
   Huge shadows creep among these mighty walls,
And on the haunting ghosts of bygone ages
   The dreamy splendour of the starlight falls.

Not Nineveh, not Babylon nor Egypt,
   In all their treasures 'neath the hungry sand,
Can show a sight so awful and majestic
   As this waste temple in this newer land.

The king that reared these mighty courts was Chaos,
   His servants, fire and elemental war ;
The Titan hands of Earthquake and of Ocean
   These granite slabs and pillars laid in store.

And lauding here the vast and living Father,
   The ages one by one have knelt and prayed,
Until the ghostly echoes of their worship
   Come back and make man's puny heart afraid.

FREDERICK G. SCOTT

147.   *Dawn*

THE immortal spirit hath no bars
   To circumscribe its dwelling-place ;
My soul hath pastured with the stars
   Upon the meadow-lands of space.

My mind and ear at times have caught,
   From realms beyond our mortal reach,
The utterance of eternal thought
   Of which all nature is the speech.

And high above the seas and lands,
   On peaks just tipped with morning light,
My dauntless spirit mutely stands
   With eagle wings outspread for flight.

DUNCAN C. SCOTT

148.   *The Reed-Player*

BY a dim shore where water darkening
   Took the last light of spring,
I went beyond the tumult, hearkening
   For some diviner thing.

Where the bats flew from the black elms like leaves,
   Over the ebon pool
Brooded the bittern's cry, as one that grieves
   Lands ancient, bountiful.

   220

DUNCAN C. SCOTT

I saw the fire-flies shine below the wood
　Above the shallows dank,
As Uriel from some great altitude,
　The planets rank on rank.

And now unseen along the shrouded mead
　One went under the hill ;
He blew a cadence on his mellow reed,
　That trembled and was still.

It seemed as if a line of amber fire
　Had shot the gathered dusk,
As if had blown a wind from ancient Tyre
　Laden with myrrh and musk.

He gave his luring note amid the fern
　Its enigmatic fall,
Haunted the hollow dusk with golden turn
　And argent interval.

I could not know the message that he bore,
　The springs of life from me
Hidden ; his incommunicable lore
　As much a mystery.

And as I followed far the magic player
　He passed the maple wood,
And when I passed the stars had risen there,
　And there was solitude.

DUNCAN C. SCOTT

149.   *The Fifteenth of April*

PALLID saffron glows the broken stubble,
    Brimmed with silver lie the ruts,
        Purple the ploughed hill ;
Down a sluice with break and bubble
        Hollow falls the rill ;
Falls and spreads and searches,
    Where, beyond the wood,
Starts a group of silver birches,
    Bursting into bud.

Under Venus sings the vesper sparrow,
    Down a path of rosy gold
        Floats the slender moon ;
Ringing from the rounded barrow
        Rolls the robin's tune ;
Lighter than the robin ; hark !
    Quivering silver-strong
From the field a hidden shore-lark
    Shakes his sparkling song.

Now the dewy sounds begin to dwindle,
    Dimmer grow the burnished rills,
        Breezes creep and halt,
Soon the guardian night shall kindle
        In the violet vault,
All the twinkling tapers
    Touched with steady gold,
Burning through the lawny vapours
    Where they float and fold.

222

DUNCAN C. SCOTT

150.   *For Remembrance*

IT would be sweet to think when we are old
  Of all the pleasant days that came to pass,
    That here we took the berries from the grass,
There charmed the bees with pans, and smoke unrolled,
And spread the melon-nets when nights were cold,
    Or pulled the blood-root in the underbrush,
    And marked the singing of the tawny thrush,
While all the west was broken burning gold.

And so I bind with rhymes these memories,
    As girls press pansies in the poet's leaves
And find them afterward with sweet surprise ;
Or treasure petals mingled with perfume,
    Loosing them in the days when April grieves ;
A subtle summer in the rainy room.

151.   *Autumn Song*

SING me a song of the Autumn clear,
    With the mellow days and the ruddy eves ;
Sing me a song of the ending year,
    With the piled-up sheaves.

Sing me a song of the apple bowers,
    Of the great grapes the vine-field yields,
Of the ripe peaches bright as flowers,
    And the rich hop-fields.

DUNCAN C. SCOTT

Sing me a song of the fallen mast,
  Of the sharp odour the pomace sheds,
Of the purple beets left last
  In the garden beds.

Sing me a song of the toiling bees,
  Of the long flight and the honey won,
Of the white hives under the apple-trees
  In the hazy sun.

Sing me a song of the thyme and the sage,
  Of sweet marjoram in the garden grey
Where goes my love Armitage
  Pulling the summer savory.

Sing me a song of the red deep,
  The long glow the sun leaves,
Of the swallows taking a last sleep
  In the barn eaves.

152.   *The Forsaken*

                        I

        ONCE in the winter,
          Out on a lake
        In the heart of the north-land,
        Far from the fort
        And far from the hunters,
        A Chippewa woman
        With her sick baby,

DUNCAN C. SCOTT

Crouched in the last hours
Of a great storm.
Frozen and hungry
She fished through the ice
With a line of the twisted
Bark of the cedar,
And a rabbit-bone hook
Polished and barbed ;
Fished with the bare hook
All through the wild day,
Fished and caught nothing ;
While the young chieftain
Tugged at her breasts,
Or slept in the lacings
Of the warm tickanegan.
All the lake surface
Streamed with the hissing
Of millions of ice-flakes,
Hurled by the wind ;
Behind her the round
Of a lonely island
Roared like a fire
With the voice of the storm
In the deeps of the cedars.
Valiant, unshaken,
She took of her own flesh,
Baited the fish-hook,
Drew in a grey-trout,
Drew in his fellow,
Heaped them beside her,

DUNCAN C. SCOTT

Dead in the snow.
Valiant, unshaken,
She faced the long distance,
Wolf-haunted and lonely,
Sure of her goal
And the life of her dear one ;
Tramped for two days,
On the third morning,
Saw the strong bulk
Of the Fort by the river,
Saw the wood-smoke
Hang soft in the spruces,
Heard the keen yelp
Of the ravenous huskies
Fighting for whitefish :
Then she had rest.

II

Years and years after,
When she was old and withered,
When her son was an old man
And his children filled with vigour,
They came in their northern tour on the verge of
    winter,
To an island in a lonely lake.
There one night they camped, and on the morrow
Gathered their kettles and birch-bark
Their rabbit-skin robes and their mink-traps,
Launched their canoes and slunk away through the
    islands,

226

Left her alone for ever.
Without a word of farewell,
Because she was old and useless,
Like a paddle broken and warped,
Or a pole that was splintered.
Then, without a sigh,
Valiant, unshaken,
She smoothed her dark locks under her kerchief,
Composed her shawl in state,
Then folded her hands ridged with sinews and corded
    with veins,
Folded them across her breasts spent with the nourish-
    ing of children,
Gazed at the sky past the tops of the cedars,
Saw two spangled nights arise out of the twilight,
Saw two days go by filled with the tranquil sunshine,
Saw, without pain, or dread, or even a moment of
    longing :
Then on the third great night there came thronging
    and thronging
Millions of snowflakes out of a windless cloud ;
They covered her close with a beautiful crystal shroud,
Covered her deep and silent.
But in the frost of the dawn,
Up from the life below,
Rose a column of breath
Through a tiny cleft in the snow,
Fragile, delicately drawn,
Wavering with its own weakness,
In the wilderness a sign of the spirit,

Persisting still in the sight of the sun
Till day was done.
Then all light was gathered up by the hand of God and
Hid in His breast,
Then there was born a silence deeper than silence,
Then she had rest.

153. *The House of the Broken-Hearted*

IT is dark to the outward seeming,
  Wherever its walls may rise,
Where the meadows are adreaming,
    Under the open skies,
    Where at ebb the great world lies,
      Dim as a sea uncharted,
    Round the house of sorrow,
      The house of the broken-hearted.

It is dark in the midst of the city,
  Where the world flows deep and strong,
Where the coldest thing is pity,
    Where the heart wears out ere long,
    Where the plough-share of wrath and of wrong
      Trenches a ragged furrow,
    Round the house of the broken-hearted,
      The house of sorrow.

But while the world goes unheeding
  The tenant that holds the lease,
Or fancies him grieving and pleading
    For the thing which it calls peace,

228

DUNCAN C. SCOTT

There has come what shall never cease
  Till there shall come no morrow
To the house of the broken-hearted,
  The house of sorrow.

There is peace no pleasure can jeopard,
  It is so sure and deep,
And there, in the guise of a shepherd,
  God doth him keep ;
  He leads His belovèd sheep
    To fold, when the day is departed,
  In the house of sorrow,
    The house of the broken-hearted.

154.   *The Half-Breed Girl*

SHE is free of the trap and the paddle,
  The portage and the trail,
But something behind her savage life
  Shines like a fragile veil.

Her dreams are undiscovered,
  Shadows trouble her breast,
When the time for resting cometh
  Then least is she at rest.

Oft in the morns of winter
  When she visits the rabbit snares,
An appearance floats in the crystal air
  Beyond the balsam firs.

DUNCAN C. SCOTT

Oft in the summer mornings
    When she strips the nets of fish,
The smell of the dripping net-twine
    Gives to her heart a wish.

But she cannot learn the meaning
    Of the shadows in her soul,
The lights that break and gather,
    The clouds that part and roll.

The reek of rock-built cities,
    Where her fathers dwelt of yore,
The gleam of loch and shealing,
    The mist on the moor,

Frail traces of kindred kindness,
    Of feud by hill and strand,
The heritage of an age-long life
    In a legendary land.

She wakes in the stifling wigwam,
    Where the air is heavy and wild,
She fears for something or nothing
    With the heart of a frightened child.

She sees the stars turn slowly
    Past the tangle of the poles,
Through the smoke of the dying embers,
    Like the eyes of dead souls.

DUNCAN C. SCOTT

Her heart is shaken with longing
    For the strange still years,
For what she knows and knows not,
    For the wells of ancient tears.

A voice calls from the rapids,
    Deep, careless, and free,
A voice that is larger than her life
    Or than her death shall be.

She covers her face with her blanket,
    Her fierce soul hates her breath,
As it cries with a sudden passion
    For life or death.

155.   *A Summer Storm*

LAST night a storm fell on the world
    From height of drouth and heat,
The surly clouds for weeks were furled,
    The air could only sway and beat,

The beetles clattered at the blind,
    The hawks fell twanging from the sky,
The west unrolled a feathery wind,
    And the night fell sullenly.

A storm leaped roaring from its lair,
    Like the shadow of doom,
The poignard lightning searched the air,
    The thunder ripped the shattered gloom,

DUNCAN C. SCOTT

The rain came down with a roar like fire,
  Full-voiced and clamorous and deep,
The weary world had its heart's desire,
  And fell asleep.

And now in the morning early
  The clouds are sailing by ;
Clearly, oh ! so clearly,
  The distant mountains lie.

The wind is very mild and slow,
  The clouds obey his will,
They part and part and onward go,
  Travelling together still.

'Tis very sweet to be alive
  On a morning that 's so fair,
For nothing seems to stir or strive
  In the unconscious air.

A tawny thrush is in the wood
  Ringing so wild and free ;
Only one bird has a blither mood—
  The whitethroat on the tree.

DUNCAN C. SCOTT

156.   *A Little Song*

THE sunset in the rosy west
  Burned soft and high ;
A shore-lark fell like a stone to his nest
  In the waving rye.

A wind came over the garden beds
  From the dreamy lawn,
The pansies nodded their purple heads,
  The poppies began to yawn.

One pansy said, ' It is only sleep,
  Only his gentle breath ; '
But a rose lay strewn in a snowy heap,
  For the rose it was only death.

Heigho ! we've only one life to live,
  And only one death to die :
Good-morrow, new world! have you nothing to give?
  Good-bye, old world—good-bye !

157.   *The End of the Day*

I HEAR the bells at eventide
  Peal slowly one by one,
Near and far off they break and glide,
  Across the stream float faintly beautiful
  The antiphonal bells of Hull ;
The day is done, done, done,
  The day is done.

DUNCAN C. SCOTT

The dew has gathered in the flowers
    Like tears from some unconscious deep,
The swallows whirl around the towers,
    And light runs out beyond the long cloud bars,
    And leaves the single stars ;
'Tis time for sleep, sleep, sleep,
    'Tis time for sleep.

The hermit thrush begins again,
    Timorous eremite,
That song of risen tears and pain,
    As if the one he loved was far away ;
    ' Alas ! another day—'
' And now Good-night, Good-Night,'
    ' Good-Night.'

JOHN S. THOMSON

158.   *An Orient Maid*

I WATCHED her tie her sandals on
   With ribbons soft as her dark hair,
The while her robe of spotless lawn
    Moved to the toyings of the air.

And when her languorous eyelids fell,—
    With purest pearl tints softly dyed,—
The dimpled smiles on her cheeks tell
    What thoughts in her sweet memory hide.

From rounded shoulder to the tips
   Of tapering fingers, pinkly bright,
And in the curve of her rose lips,
   Nature had lavished line and light.

A zone with sapphires sprinkled o'er
   Caught up the flowings of her gown ;
And pendent, jewelled charms she wore,
   To her warm bosom reaching down.

I wondered if on lavender,
   Or silken pillows, perfume-filled,
Or bed of aromatic fir,
   She slept through nights, by love's dreams stilled.

159.   *Transformed*

'TWAS in the purple-flow'ring month we met,
   And I had gathered fleurs-de-lis for her ;
   And sought the dim wood where the fern leaves stir
   To find an orchis, fringed and sweet and wet ;
These in her simple joy she coyly set
   Among her tresses ;—but I knew her not ;
   Some passing wind a sylph or nymph had brought.

And ere I sighed or spoke a vain regret,
   She led me to a green and shadowy grove,
   Where fallow-deer, large eyed, did shyly rove ;—
   And on a bank of thyme we two did sit ;
Words were forgotten ; in her wide blue eyes
   I read some symbol language, though my wit
   Hád passed away. I dwelt in Paradise.

235

JOHN S. THOMSON

160. *An Autumn Wind*

A TRUCE with cares and labours! I have cried;
  And traced the sweet winds to the barley field,
To watch the strong browned reapers, joyous wield
Their curved and twinkling sickles side by side.
And where the harvest valley opened wide,
  A breeze fell down among the rip'ning grain,
  Driving the golden waves across the plain,
And dipping in the nooks, where fieldlarks hide.

Brave with its gambol, still it went until
It waved the loosestrifes' ribbons o'er the hill,
  And spilled the dazzling sunset from the flow'rs.
Within a forest, then it hid at night;
  To waken when the morning filled the bow'rs
With fragrance, and with floods of violet light.

161. *Along the Way*

A SPARROW on a flow'ry hedge
  Melts all his soul in song,—the pledge
    Of the supernal year;
And purple morning-glories lift
To the sun's rays a cooling gift
    Of nectar-wine for cheer.
  Like fields of wind-tossed stars, the marguerites
      Tremble in lone retreats.
      The briar roses pink
Invite the bee to musk dew-drink;
236

And thrushes in the dim wood sing
   Wild strains, with which the leafy coverts ring.
     On olive lily-pads the gold
     Of new-blown petals is unrolled,
   And bobolincolns trail along
     A tinkling chain of song.

JAMES E. CALDWELL

162.   *Peccavi*

HERE 'neath my father's ample roof,
   The blue and bending sky,
A child, I lived in happiness,
   Unmindful of the Why.

Far o'er the Earth the mystic charm
   Of Nature softly fell
By day, at night the wonderment
   Which lips can never tell.

And human love and kindly speech
   Were blent with human tears ;
And hearkening oft there faintly came
   The music of the spheres.

But ah ! too common seem'd my lot ;
   Weird travellers' tales I heard
Of fairy lands and magic towers,
   And realms of grief unstirred.

JAMES E. CALDWELL

Unminded now the glorious sun
  Might bathe the Earth in light,
No more the rapture of the hills
  Did sanctify the night.

O'er all the household hopes and tasks
  Was writ Unclean, Unclean ;
Upon the idly rusting plough
  My nerveless hand did lean.

Deep discontent did gnaw my heart,
  Fast bound to grossest needs ;
While far away I heard the call
  Of winged and fiery steeds.

' Far hence I go,' no hand restrained,
  Rich largess too I bore
Of ruddy blood and supple limbs,
  And sought that mystic shore.

How shall I speak of wasted years,
  Of tantalizing quest,
Of desert wind that inly sears
  The disenchanted breast.

A land unblest by chastening law,
  Fantastically blent,
Of poppied dreams, and tilted seas,
  And meteors cold and spent.

238

JAMES E. CALDWELL

There 'mid the wreck of futile dreams
   And giddy hours, the swine—
Basest of all my former years—
   Alone, alone were mine.

Cold, grey, yet clearing like the dawn
   After a night of mirth,
Came to my heart the piercing cry,
   Ah ! why scorned I the Earth !

Myriad, uncounted, infinite,
   The chisel-marks it bears ;
Myriad, uncounted, infinite,
   Its upward mounting stairs.

Bread and to spare who toils shall have,
   And blesses with his thought ;
The friendly door, the garment fair,
   The ring with jewels wrought.

' Peccavi,'—O what health doth spring
   From that astringent word !
Scarce uttered till beside me sang
   A tiny fearless bird.

Beside me crunched the crowding swine,
   With many an uncouth call ;
Why grudged I then my service while
   In turn man claim'd their all ?

239

JAMES E. CALDWELL

Far on my way I fared that eve,
  Stripped, penitent, and worn,
But in my heart a feeling surged—
  I am not all forlorn.

Serve will I and endow myself
  With all I once did scorn;
And smite with sharp and willing too
  The thistle and the thorn.

So came I to my father's house,
  But all the place was still;
I waited at the silent door,
  · Irresolute of will.

My father's staff hung by the door,
  All mildewed was the crook;
A terror fill'd my trembling frame,
  So fearful did it look!

Out from the door then slowly stept
  My brother, bent and grey;
Till then I had not dream'd what years
  Had swiftly passed away!

Half dazed he stood and scann'd me o'er;
  At last he caught the clue;
With outstretched hand he slowly spake,
  'Ah, brother, is it you?'

JAMES E. CALDWELL

Slowly from out that awful chill
 Of fear my spirit stirred,
And all the melancholy tale
 In voiceless grief I heard.

Now through the silent rooms I range,
 And o'er the distant hills ;
But something in the vanished past
 No more my spirit fills.

And never more my father's voice
 Comes with insistent tone ;
And I, alas ! am all too free
 To tread my path alone.

But yet the days are fill'd with sun,
 The Earth with chemic force ;
From unseen founts the rivers run
 To seek their ocean source.

And slowly from the grief and loss
 My spirit upward springs,
And seeks the precious grain of truth
 From endless winnowings.

Though on my father's face no more
 I gaze with mortal eye,
Still o'er the old familiar scene
 His blessing seems to lie.

And still remain all powers which were
   In him personified,—
Strength, goodness, wisdom, charity,
   Forgiveness free and wide.

And from him still proceeds a force
   Which never shall return,
With vaster, nobler meaning charged,
   In purer love to burn.

163.   *Ottawa*

G RANDEUR is written on thy throne,
   Beauty encompasseth thy mien ;
The glory of the North alone,
   Is thine, O Ottawa, my Queen.

Here as the years of promise roll
   Shall gather all a nation's pride ;
The great of intellect and soul
   Shall build a city, vast and wide.

Here shall the sculptor's vision stand
   For ever caught in burnished bronze ;
Roof, tower, and column, nobly plann'd,
   Shall greet the future's mystic dawns.

Here shall the plunging torrent's wrath
   Strange kindness to the toiler show ;
Here o'er the steel, the watery path,
   The East and West commingling flow,

JAMES E. CALDWELL

Here shall the human wants that lead
   To hunger, thirst, and sore distress,
Be met before their cruel need
   By trade shorn of its sordidness.

Not here shall shelter foul disease
   In sunless lairs bereft of sky ;
Nor Death be hidden in the lees
   Of fountains which man's needs supply

A press shall flourish, kind but grave,
   Well recking of the trusts they bear ;
Unbought of wealth, unawed by knave,
   The truth shall modestly declare.

Like honeyed flowers that call the bees,
   The hoarded lore of every age
Shall gather gladsome companies
   Of lovers of the printed page.

Here shall the code of Righteousness
   Be set to common speech once more,
And noble deeds shall daily bless
   Of which men only dreamed before.

And here the ancient hills appeal
   To all that most endures in man,
Rebuking hate and strident zeal,
   For ah, how brief our breathing span !

Beloved of cities thou shalt be—
   Wise, fair, strong, joyous and serene—
Once more accept my fealty—
   My love, O Ottawa, my Queen !

ETHELWYN WETHERALD

The Wind of Death

THE wind of death that softly blows
The last warm petal from the rose,
The last dry leaf from off the tree,
To-night has come to breathe on me.

There was a time I learned to hate
As weaker mortals learn to love ;
The passion held me fixed as fate,
Burned in my veins early and late ;
But now a wind falls from above,
The wind of death, that silently
Enshroudeth friend and enemy.

There was a time my soul was thrilled
By keen ambition's whip and spur ;
My master forced me where he willed,
And with his power my life was filled,
But now the old-time pulses stir
How faintly in the wind of death !
That bloweth lightly as a breath.

And once, but once, at Love's dear feet,
I yielded strength, and life, and heart ;
His look turned bitter into sweet,
His smile made all the world complete ;
The wind blows loves like leaves apart,
The wind of death, that tenderly
Is blowing 'twixt my love and me.
244

ETHELWYN WETHERALD

O wind of death, that darkly blows
Each separate ship of human woes
Far out on a mysterious sea,
I turn, I turn my face to thee.

165.   *The Plowman*

I HEARD the plowman sing in the wind,
  And sing right merrily,
As down in the cold of the sunless mould
  The grasses buried he.

And now the grasses sing in the wind,
  Merrily do they sing ;
While down in the cold of the sunless mould
  Is the plowman slumbering.

166.   *The House of the Trees*

OPE your doors and take me in,
  Spirit of the wood ;
Wash me clean of dust and din,
  Clothe me in your mood.

Take me from the noisy light
  To the sunless peace,
Where at midday standeth Night
  Singing Toil's release.

245

All your dusky twilight stores
   To my senses give ;
Take me in and lock the doors,
   Show me how to live.

Lift your leafy roof for me,
   Part your yielding walls,
Let me wander lingeringly
   Through your scented halls.

Ope your doors and take me in,
   Spirit of the wood ;
Take me, make me next of kin
   To your leafy brood.

167.   *Moonlight*

WHEN I see the ghost of night
   Stealing through my window-pane,
Silken sleep and silver light
   Struggle for my soul in vain ;
Silken sleep all balmily
   Breathes upon my lids oppressed,
Till I sudden start and see
   Ghostly fingers on my breast.

White and skyey visitant,
   Bringing beauty such as stings
All my inner soul to pant
   After undiscovered things,

ETHELWYN WETHERALD

Spare me this consummate pain !
  Silken weavings intercreep
Round my senses once again,
  I am mortal—let me sleep.

168.   *The Blind Man*

THE blind man at his window-bars
  Stands in the morning dewy dim ;
The lily-footed dawn, the stars
  That wait for it, are naught to him.

And naught to his unseeing eyes
  The brownness of a sunny plain,
Where worn and drowsy August lies,
  And wakens but to sleep again.

And naught to him a greening slope,
  That yearns up to the heights above,
And naught the leaves of May, that ope
  As softly as the eyes of love.

And naught to him the branching aisles,
  Athrong with woodland worshippers,
And naught the fields where summer smiles
  Among her sunburned labourers.

The way a trailing streamlet goes,
  The barefoot grasses on its brim,
The dew a flower cup o'erflows
  With silent joy, are hid from him.

ETHELWYN WETHERALD

To him no breath of Nature calls ;
  Upon his desk his work is laid ;
He looks up at the dingy walls,
  And listens to the voice of Trade.

169.   *Out of Doors*

IN the urgent solitudes
  Lies the spur to larger moods ;
In the friendship of the trees
Dwell all sweet serenities.

170.   *The Pasture Field*

WHEN spring has burned
  The ragged robe of winter, stitch by stitch,
And deftly turned
  To moving melody the wayside ditch,
The pale-green pasture field behind the bars
Is goldened o'er with dandelion stars.

When summer keeps
  Quick pace with sinewy, white-shirted arms,
And daily steeps
  In sunny splendour all her spreading farms,
The pasture field is flooded foamy white
With daisy faces looking at the light.

248

ETHELWYN WETHERALD

When autumn lays
   Her golden wealth upon the forest floor,
And all the days
   Look backward at the days that went before,
A pensive company, the asters, stand,
Their blue eyes brightening the pasture land.

When winter lifts
   A sounding trumpet to his strenuous lips,
And shapes the drifts
   To curves of transient loveliness, he slips
Upon the pasture's ineffectual brown
A swan-soft vestment delicate as down.

171.   *The Indigo Bird*

WHEN I see,
      High on the tip-top twig of a tree,
Something blue by the breezes stirred,
But so far up that the blue is blurred,
So far up that no green leaf flies
'Twixt its blue and the blue of the skies,
Then I know, ere a note be heard,
That is naught but the Indigo bird.

Blue on the branch and blue in the sky,
And naught between but the breezes high,
And naught so blue by the breezes stirred
As the deep, deep blue of the Indigo bird.

249

ETHELWYN WETHERALD

When I hear
A song like a bird laugh, blithe and clear,
As though of some airy jest he had heard
The last and the most delightful word,
A laugh as fresh in the August haze
As it was in the full-voiced April days,
Then I know that my heart is stirred
By the laugh-like song of the Indigo bird.

Joy in the branch and joy in the sky,
And naught between but the breezes high ;
And naught so glad on the breezes heard
As the gay, gay note of the Indigo bird.

JEAN BLEWETT

172. *She just keeps House for Me*

SHE is so winsome and so wise
She sways us at her will,
And oft the question will arise,
What mission does she fill ?
And so I say with pride untold,
And love beyond degree,
This woman with the heart of gold,
She just keeps house for me—
For me,—
She just keeps house for me.

JEAN BLEWETT

A full content dwells in her face,
  She 's quite in love with life,
And for a title, wears with grace
    The sweet, old-fashioned ' Wife ' ;
      And so I say with pride untold,
        And love beyond degree,
      This woman with the heart of gold
        She just keeps house for me—
                For me,—
      She just keeps house for me.

What though I toil from morn till night,
  What though I weary grow,
A spring of love and dear delight
  Doth ever softly flow ;
      And so I say with pride untold,
        And love beyond degree,
      The woman with the heart of gold
        She just keeps house for me.

Our children climb upon her knee
  And lie upon her breast,
And ah ! her mission seems to me
  The highest and the best ;
      And so I say with pride untold,
        And love beyond degree,
      This woman with the heart of gold
        She just keeps house for me.

JEAN BLEWETT

173.   *Spring*

OH, the frozen valley and frozen hill make a coffin wide and deep,
And the dead river lies, all its laughter stilled within it, fast asleep.

The trees that have played with the merry thing, and freighted its breast with leaves,—
Give never a murmur or sigh of woe—they are dead—no dead thing grieves.

No carol of love from a song-bird's throat; the world lies naked and still,
For all things tender, and all things sweet, have been touched by the gruesome chill.

Not a flower—a blue forget-me-not, a wild rose, or jasmine soft—
To lay its bloom on the dead river's lips, that have kissed them all so oft.

But look! a ladder is spanning the space 'twixt earth and the sky beyond,
A ladder of gold for the Maid of Grace—the strong, the subtle, the fond!

Spring, with a mantle made of the gold held close in a sunbeam's heart,
Thrown over her shoulders bonnie and bare—see the sap in the great trees start!

252

JEAN BLEWETT

Where the hem of this flowing garment trails, see the
  glow, the colour bright,
A stirring and spreading of something fair—the dawn
  is chasing the night !

Spring, with all love and all dear delights pulsing in
  every vein,
The old earth knows her, and thrills to her touch, as
  she claims her own again.

Spring, with the hyacinths filling her lap and violet
  seeds in her hair,
With the crocus hiding its satin head in her bosom
  warm and fair ;

Spring, with the daffodils at her feet and pansies
  abloom in her eyes ;
Spring, with enough of God in herself to make the
  dead arise !

For see, as she bends o'er the coffin deep—the frozen
  valley and hill—
The dead river stirs,—ah, that lingering kiss is making
  its heart to thrill.

And then as she closer and closer leans, it slips from
  its snowy shroud,
Frightened a moment, then rushing away, calling and
  laughing aloud !

The hill where she rested is all abloom, the wood is
  green as of old,
And wakened birds are striving to send their songs to
  the Gates of Gold.

253

JEAN BLEWETT

174.   *Margaret*

HER eyes—upon a summer's day
God's skies are not more blue than they.

Her hair—you've seen a sunbeam bold
Made up of just such threads of gold.

Her cheek—the leaf which nearest grows
The dewy heart of June's red rose.

Her mouth—full lipped, and subtly sweet
As brier drowned in summer heat.

Her heart—December's chill and snow ;
Heaven pity me, who love her so !

E. PAULINE JOHNSON

175.   *The Song my Paddle sings*

WEST wind, blow from your prairie nest,
Blow from the mountains, blow from the west.
The sail is idle, the sailor too ;
Oh ! wind of the west, we wait for you.
Blow, blow !
I have wooed you so,
But never a favour you bestow.
You rock your cradle the hills between,—
But scorn to notice my white lateen.

E. PAULINE JOHNSON

I stow the sail and unship the mast;
I wooed you long, but my wooing 's past;
My paddle will lull you into rest;
O drowsy wind of the drowsy west,
Sleep, sleep!
By your mountains steep,
Or down where the prairie grasses sweep,
Now fold in slumber your laggard wings,
For soft is the song my paddle sings.

August is laughing across the sky,
Laughing while paddle, canoe and I
Drift, drift,
Where the hills uplift
On either side of the current swift.

The river rolls in its rocky bed,
My paddle is plying its way ahead,
Dip, dip,
When the waters flip
In foam as over their breast we slip.

And oh, the river runs swifter now;
The eddies circle about my bow;
Swirl, swirl,
How the ripples curl
In many a dangerous pool awhirl!

And far to forward the rapids roar,
Fretting their margin for evermore;
Dash, dash,
With a mighty crash,
They seethe and boil and bound and splash.

E. PAULINE JOHNSON

Be strong, O Paddle ! be brave, Canoe !
The reckless waves you must plunge into.
Reel, reel,
On your trembling keel,
But never a fear my craft will feel.

We've raced **the rapids ; we're far** ahead ;
The river slips through its silent bed.
Sway, sway,
As the bubbles spray
And fall in tinkling tunes away.

And up on the hills against the sky,
A fir-tree rocking its lullaby
Swings, swings,
Its emerald wings,
Swelling the song that my paddle sings.

176.   *The Cattle Country*

UP the dusk-enfolded prairie,
    Footfalls soft and sly,
Velvet cushioned, wild and wary ;
    Then—the coyote's cry.

Rush of hoofs and roar and rattle ;
    Beasts of blood and breed—
Twenty thousand frightened cattle ;
    Then—the wild stampede.

256

E. PAULINE JOHNSON

Pliant lasso, circling wider,
　　With the frenzied flight ;
Loping horse and cursing rider
　　Plunging through the night.

Rim of dawn the darkness losing,
　　Trail of blackened loam,
Perfume of the sage brush oozing
　　On the air like foam.

Foothills to the Rockies lifting,
　　Brown, and blue, and green ;
Warm Alberta sunlight drifting
　　Over leagues between.

That 's the country of the ranges,
　　Plain, and prairie-land ;
And the God who never changes
　　Holds it in His hand.

177.　　　　　*Harvest Time*

PILLOWED and hushed on the silent plain,
Wrapped in her mantle of golden grain,

Wearied of pleasuring weeks away,
Summer is lying asleep to-day,—

Where winds come sweet from the wild-rose briers
And the smoke of the far-off prairie fires.

Yellow her hair as the golden-rod,
And brown her cheeks as the prairie sod ;

Purple her eyes as the mists that dream
At the edge of some laggard sun-drowned stream ;

But over their depths the lashes sweep,
For Summer is lying to-day asleep.

The north wind kisses her rosy mouth,
His rival frowns in the far-off south,

And comes caressing her sunburnt cheek,
And Summer awakes for one short week,—

Awakes and gathers her wealth of grain,
Then sleeps and dreams for a year again.

178.   *Guard of the Eastern Gate*

HALIFAX sits on her hills by the sea
    In the might of her pride,—
Invincible, terrible, beautiful, she
    With a sword at her side.

To right and to left of her, battlements rear
    And fortresses frown ;
While she sits on her throne without favour or fear,
    With her cannon as crown.

Coast-guard and sentinel, watch of the weal
    Of a nation she keeps;
But her hand is encased in a gauntlet of steel,
    And her thunder but sleeps.

179.   *Lullaby of the Iroquois*

LITTLE brown baby-bird, lapped in your nest,
    Wrapped in your nest,
    Strapped in your nest,
Your straight little cradle-board rocks you to rest;
    Its hands are your nest,
    Its bands are your nest;
It swings from the down-bending branch of the oak;
You watch the camp flame, and the curling grey smoke;
But, oh, for your pretty black eyes sleep is best,—
Little brown baby of mine, go to rest.

Little brown baby-bird swinging to sleep,
    Winging to sleep,
    Singing to sleep,
Your wonder-black eyes that so wide open keep,
    Shielding their sleep,
    Unyielding to sleep,
The heron is homing, the plover is still,
The night-owl calls from his haunt on the hill,
Afar the fox barks, afar the stars peep,—
Little brown baby of mine, go to sleep.

ARTHUR STRINGER

180. *Northern Pines*

I PASS where the pines for Christmas
  Stand thick in the crowded street,
Where the groves of Dream and Silence
  Are paced by feverish feet.

And far through the rain and the street-cries
  My homesick heart goes forth
To the pine-clad hills of childhood,
  To the dark and tender North.

And I see the glooming pine-lands,
  And I thrill to the Northland cold,
Where the sunset falls in silence
  On the hills of gloom and gold !

And the still dusk woods close round me,
  And I know the waiting eyes
Of my North, as a child's, are tender,
  As a sorrowing mother's, wise !

181. *On a Child's Portrait*

DEEP in the fluted hollow of its shells
  Dimly some echo of the ocean dwells.

Still in September's fruitage, mellow-cored,
The filtered sweets of golden noons are stored.

And shimmering on a blue-bird's migrant wings
Some poignant touch of June's lost azure clings.

ARTHUR STRINGER

Still in the rustling sheaf to-day there gleams
The lingering gold of April's vanished dreams.

Still in the cell of one autumnal bee
I find lost summer in epitome.

And all that better life that I would lead,
Writ small in this, one childish face, I read.

182.   *Non Omnis Moriar*

IN the teeth of the Word that bars my track,
  In the swirl of the Ebb that sucks me down,
In the face of the storm that flings me back
  On the wrath of a Deep grown mountainous-walled,
I, *I*, tide by tide, and tack by tack,
  As far as the chains will let me free—
I threading a course unbuoyed and black,
  And feeling the Night where fanged rocks frown,
Ere the last spar sail, shall have somehow crawled
  To that Port whence shone no light for me ;
Where, wrecked, if you will, but unappalled,
  I shall know I am stronger than my Sea !

183.   *Keats*

ALL over-thumbed, dog-eared, and stained with
    grass,
All bleached with sun and time, and eloquent
Of afternoons in golden-houred romance,
You turn them o'er, those comrade books of mine,
And idly ask me what I think of Keats.

ARTHUR STRINGER

But let me likewise question you round whom
The clangour of the Market sweeps and clings ;
In Summer toward the murmurous close of June
Have you e'er walked some dusty meadow path
That faced the sun and quivered in the heat,
And as you brushed through grass and daisy drift,
Found glowing on some sunburnt little knoll
One deep, red, over-ripe wild strawberry ?—
The sweetest fruit beneath Canadian skies,
And in that sun-bleached field the only touch
Of lustrous colour to redeem the Spring—
The flame-red passion of life's opulence
Grown over-sweet and soon ordained to death !

And have you ever caught up in your hand
That swollen globe of soft deliciousness ?
You notice first the colour, richly red ;
And then the odour, strangely sweet and sharp,
And last of all, you crush its ruddy core
Against your lips, till colour, taste, and scent
Might make your stained mouth stop the murmur ;
    ' This
The very heart of Summer that I crush ! '
So poignant through its lusciousness it seems !
Then what 's the need, Old Friend, of foolish words :
I've shown you now just what I think of Keats.

ARTHUR WEIR

184. *The Two Troopers*

SWIFT troopers twain ride side by side
   Throughout life's long campaign.
They make a jest of all man's pride,
And oh, the havoc! As they ride
   They cannot count their slain.

The one is young and debonair,
   And laughing swings his blade!
The Zephyrs toss his golden hair,
His eyes are blue ; he is so fair
   He seems a masking maid.

The other is a warrior grim,
   Dark as a midnight storm ;
There is no man can cope with him,
We shrink and tremble in each limb
   Before his awful form.

Yet though men fear the sombre foe
   More than the gold-tressed youth,
The boy with every careless blow
More than the trooper grim lays low,
   And causes earth more ruth.

Keener his mocking sword doth prove
   Than flame or winter's breath :
Men bear his wounds to the realm above,
For the little trooper's name is Love,
   His comrade 's only Death.

PHILLIPS STEWART

Hope

IN shadowy calm the boat
　Sleeps by the dreaming oar,
The green hills are afloat
　Beside the silver shore.

Youth hoists the white-winged sail,
　Love takes the longing oar—
The oft-told fairy tale
　Beside the silver shore.

Soft lip to lip, and heart
　To heart, and hand to hand,
And wistful eyes depart
　Unto another strand.

And lovely as a star
　They tremble o'er the wave,
With eager wings afar
　Unto the joys they crave.

In a sweet trance they fare
　Unto the wind and rain,
With wind-tossed waves of hair,
　And ne'er return again.

And at the drifting side,
　Changed faces in the deep
They see, and changing tide,
　Like phantoms in a sleep.

PHILLIPS STEWART

Slow hands furl the torn sail
    Without one silver gleam,
And sad, and wan, and pale,
    They gaze into a dream.

186.   *Freedom*

From " Lines to my Mother "

TRUE greatness is the struggle to be free,
    And he who would be truly great must bear
A thorny heart for lovely Freedom's sake.
Ignominy and gloom, curses, blind lies,
The scorn of little minds, the bitter hemlock bowl,
Are all he wins in life.   Hail, noble Queen !
Thy reign is growing larger every hour.
Hail to the light of thine eternal brow !
The little lights must fade in thee, as moths
Dissolve in flame—the little lights must die.
Is it a sin to doubt the past, that speaks
The darkened mind ?   Hail, light unquenchable !
From Thee priestcraft and superstition skulk
Into oblivion, and caves of night,
And mumbling mouths that mourn the outworn past.
The rights and lives of men are but half built,
When inhumanity hath greater power
Than love ; what wonder that the world is full
Of clanking chains, and rayless cells of gloom !

ANONYMOUS

187.   *The Riders of the Plains*

WE wake the prairie echoes with
    The ever-welcome sound,
' Ring out the boot and saddle ' till
    Its stirring notes resound.
Our horses toss their bridled heads
    And chafe against the reins ;
Ring out, ring out the marching call
    Of the Riders of the Plains.

Full many a league o'er prairie wild
    Our trackless path must be,
And round it roam the fiercest tribes
    Of Blackfoot and of Cree ;
But danger from their savage bands
    Our dauntless heart disdains,
That heart which bears the helmet up
    Of the Riders of the Plains.

The thunderstorm sweeps o'er our way,
    But onward still we go ;
We scale the rugged mountain range,
    Descend the valleys low ;
We face the dread Saskatchewan,
    Brimmed high with heavy rains ;
With all his might he cannot check
    The Riders of the Plains.
266

ANONYMOUS

We muster but three hundred
  In all this great lone land,
Which stretches o'er the continent
  To where the Rockies stand ;
But not one heart doth falter,
  No coward voice complains,
That few, too few, in numbers are
  The Riders of the Plains.

Our mission is to plant the rule
  Of Britain's freedom here,
Restrain the lawless savage, and
  Protect the pioneer ;
And 'tis a proud and daring trust
  To hold these vast domains,
With but three hundred mounted men,
  The Riders of the Plains.

We bear no lifted banner,
  The soldier's care and pride ;
No waving flag leads onward
  Our horsemen when they ride ;
The sense of duty well discharged
  All idle thought sustains,
No other spur to action need
  The Riders of the Plains.

JAMES A. TUCKER

188. *Life's Shaping Moments*

THINGS we deemed greatest, looked at from the
    distance,
  Have oft had little bearing on life's course ;
The trivial (as we judge), with strange insistence,
  Doth tinge the years with gladness or remorse.

Forward we press, towards some enchanted bower
  That beckons us to come and taste its shade,
And lo ! beside our path a little flower,
  Unlooked-for, makes the farther vision fade.

To yonder great man came life's wished-for honour,
  Which neither helped or stayed him from the goal;—
But in the throng that night he gazed upon her,
  And that one glance made history for his soul !

EMILY McMANUS

189. *Manitoba*

SOFTLY the shadows of prairie-land wheat
  Ripple and riot adown to her feet ;
Murmurs all Nature with joyous acclaim,
Fragrance of summer and shimmer of flame :
Heedless she hears while the centuries slip :—
Chalice of poppy is laid on her lip.

EMILY McMANUS

Hark ! From the East comes a ravishing note,—
Sweeter was never in nightingale's throat—
Silence of centuries thrills to the song,
Singing their silence awaited so long ;
Low, yet it swells to the heaven's blue dome,
Child-lips have called the wild meadow-land ' Home ! '

Deep, as she listens, a dewy surprise
Dawns in the languor that darkens her eyes ;
Swift the red blood through her veins, in its flow,
Kindles to rapture her bosom aglow ;
Voices are calling, where silence has been,
' Look to the future, thou Mother of Men ! '

Onward and onward ! Her fertile expanse
Shakes as the tide of her children advance ;
Onward and onward ! Her blossoming floor
Yields her an opium potion no more ;
Onward ! and soon on her welcoming soil
Cities shall palpitate, myriads toil.

JEAN GRAHAM

190.   *Where Dreams are Sold*

AT the silken sign of the Poppy,
   At a shop which is never old,
Where a twilight silence lingers—
   It is there that dreams are sold.

JEAN GRAHAM

There 's the scent of Love's lost roses,
  The soft echo of childhood's laugh,
There 's the ring of empty glasses,
  For the white lips never quaff.

To the silken sign of the Poppy
  We all come when the daylight dies,
When the curfew music echoes,
  'Neath the grey of evening skies.

Just beyond the gates of sunset,
  Where the grim toll of death we pay,
We shall find the shop of dream-ware
  Where the poppies hang alway.

So we long for dusk of the twilight
  When, with wealth of no earthly gold,
We shall come where sleep-flowers cluster,
  To the shop where dreams are sold.

KATHERINE HALE

191.   *Song of Roses*

O SINGING Youth, thou wert to me
  A pink rose of expectancy !
Laughing I laid thee on my breast,
All radiant of Joy's bright quest.

Therewith, on the appointed day,
Came Life to meet me on the way ;
A gold rose gave into my hand—
The seal of strength to understand.

270

Then, like some wide transforming morn,
Soul signalled soul and love was born,
And Youth that laughs and Life that knows
Melted into one crimson rose.

. . . .

Now God alone can make complete
This little garland soft and sweet,
And give me Death's white rose of light,
For ever fresh, for ever bright,

That I may bind with cool green leaves
The flowers of Life with Death's pale sheaves,
And send them, stripped of thorn and rue,
Perfect and passionless—to you.

ALMA F. McCOLLUM

192.   *The Kissing-Gate*

THE lakelet lapped its pebbled beach
   In rhythmic ebb and flow,
Accordant with the melody
   The forest whispered low ;
The arborvitae's spicy breath
   With fragrance filled the glade,
As o'er a rustic kissing-gate
   It cast protecting shade ;
There, Love, you waited ardently
The precious toll to take from me.

ALMA F. McCOLLUM

To-day the song is softly crooned
  In minor undertone,
As through the wood I sadly stroll
  Alone, my love, alone.
An eerie wind has caught the gate
  And open flung it wide ;
O Love, I would the great Beyond
  Were just the other side !
Where we could find some restful spot
And feel the peace the world gives not.

Has Heaven glowing jasper walls,
  And golden portal tall ?
Tell me there is a forest lake,
  And glad sky over all ;
That arborvitaes thickly mass
  And waft their incense sweet
Above an olden trysting-place,
  Where we were wont to meet ;
Tell me there is a kissing-gate,
Where you, O love, my love, will wait !

ISABEL ECCLESTONE-MACKAY

193.   *Dream People*

WHERE dwell the dear dream people who fly at
    break of day ?
Their laughter sinks to silence, their faces melt away—
The only voice that lingers is the voice which bids
    them stay !

ISABEL ECCLESTONE-MACKAY

We know they wait us somewhere, safe-harboured by
the night ;
They are as real as hand or brain, as vivid as the light,
As actual as is the sun whose coming speeds their flight.

They bring the breath of summer, the autumn moon,
the sigh
That stirs the perfumed bushes as the night wind
wanders by,
And all the sweet dead sights and sounds that never
really die.

They come with tears and laughter ; they never fail
or fade—
Last night myself came dancing back a little red-
cheeked maid,
With aproned frock and braided hair and clear eyes
unafraid.

And often comes a merry lad, laughing, and tall and
tanned,
And all the old delight sweeps back—his hand upon
my hand,
With just we two alone in all the lovely, love-lit land !

Yet when we wake they leave us ! I wonder where
they stay.
And when we never wake at all shall we be just as
they—
For ever free, for ever young, beyond the touch of day?

HELEN M. MERRILL

194.   *The Canada Wind*

WHENCE bloweth the Canada wind ?
   Not out of the west, though the west winds bear
Lightsome hours and the joy of spring,
And the heavenly blue of a wild bird's wing ;
For the heart of the violet scents the air,
And the scent of the violet is all too fair
Its flowers in my hair to bind—
   The west wind is of the lea,
   And palls on the soul of me.

Whence bloweth the Canada wind ?
Oh, not from the south, for the south wind brings
Summer and dim, sweet, forest deeps,
And a bird in the wild wood hidden keeps,
And mellow songs in the green light sings ;
And flower, and song, and mystical things
My soul with dreamings blind—
   The south wind is of the sun,
   My soul is for a day undone.

Whence bloweth the Canada wind ?
Not out of the east, for the east wind chills
With its dank, grey mists and its storms of rain,
And dawn is foredooming again and again ;

HELEN M. MERRILL

Noon's dripping sky with greyness fills,
And night is black on the sodden hills,
And never a star I find—
    The east wind is of the sea,
    And drives to the heart of me.

Whence bloweth the Canada wind ?
Its path is the way to the world's white rim,
The strange white tracts of the barren zone,
Immutable, luminous, wild and lone ;
Spaces enduring through aeons dim,
Veiling the sea, and the blue sea's brim,
Striving for ever, yet never free,
Fetters which ever bind—
The Canada wind is the keen north wind,
    The wind of the secret sea,
    And quickens the soul of me.

195.   *Where no Land Lies*

WHERE no land lies,
    Far out under the cloudy skies,
Alone, adrift,
A gleam of blue in a quiet rift,
The monotonous flow
Of waves which gather, and come, and go
On for ever.

Where no land lies,
Far off, a lonely sea-gull cries,

And clouds come down
On my hair all flowing, and cool, and brown,
And in my face
The slanting rain-drops drive apace,
Ever and ever.

Where no land lies,
And only the screaming sea-gull flies,
Alone, all day,
The dull sea waste is my chosen way ;
In wind and rain
I dream mine olden dreams again,
Ever a part
Of the wilding sea's lone, passionate heart ;
In rain and wind
An idle ecstasy I find,
Where only the lonely sea-gull cries,
Where no land lies.

ROBERT W. SERVICE

196.   *The Law of the Yukon*

THIS is the law of the Yukon, and ever she makes
    it plain :
' Send not your foolish and feeble ; send me your
    strong and your sane ;
Strong for the red rage of battle ; sane, for I harry
    them sore ;
Send me men girt for the combat, men who are grit
    to the core ;

ROBERT W. SERVICE

Swift as the panther in triumph, fierce as the bear in
    defeat,
Sired of bulldog parent, steeled in the furnace heat.
Send me the best of your breeding, lend me your
    chosen ones ;
Them will I take to my bosom, them will I call my
    sons ;
Them will I gild with my treasure, them will I glut
    with my meat ;
But the others—the misfits, the failures—I trample
    under my feet ;
Dissolute, damned and despairful, crippled and palsied
    and slain,
Ye would send me the spawn of your gutters—Go !
    take back your spawn again.

' Wild and wide are my borders, stern as death is my
    sway ;
From my ruthless throne I have ruled alone for a
    million years and a day ;
Hugging my mighty treasure, waiting for man to come:
Till he swept like a turbid torrent, and after him
    swept—the scum,
The pallid pimp of the dead line, the enervate of the
    pen,
One by one I weeded them out, for all that I sought
    was—Men.
One by one I dismayed them, frightened them sore
    with my glooms ;
One by one I betrayed them unto my manifold dooms ;

Drowned them like rats in my rivers, starved them like
    curs on my plains,
Rotted the flesh that was left them, poisoned the blood
    in their veins ;
Burst with my winter upon them, searing for ever
    their sight,
Lashed them with fungus-white faces, whimpering
    wild in the night ;
Staggering wild in the storm-whirl, stumbling mad
    through the snow,
Frozen stiff in the ice-pack, brittle and bent like a bow ;
Featureless, formless, forsaken, scented by wolves in
    their flight,
Left for the wind to make music through ribs that
    are glittering white ;
Gnawing the black crust of failure, searching the pit
    of despair,
Crooking the toe in the trigger, trying to patter a
    prayer ;
Going outside with an escort, raving with lips all
    afoam ;
Writing a cheque for a million, drivelling feebly of
    home ;
Lost like a louse in the burning . . . or else in the
    tented town
Seeking a drunkard's solace, sinking and sinking down ;
Steeped in the slime at the bottom, dead to a decent
    world,
Lost 'mid the human flotsam, far on the frontier
    hurled ;

ROBERT W. SERVICE

In the camp at the bend of the river, with its dozen
    saloons aglare,
Its gambling dens a-riot, its gramophones all ablare ;
Crimped with the crimes of a city, sin-ridden and
    bridled with lies
In the hush of my mountained vastness, so natheless
    I suffer them thrive,
Crushing my Weak in their clutches, that only my
    Strong may survive.

' But the others, the men of my mettle, the men who
    would 'stablish my fame,
Unto its ultimate issue, winning me honour, not shame ;
Searching my uttermost valleys, fighting each step as
    they go,
Shooting the wrath of my rapids, scaling my ramparts
    of snow ;
Ripping the guts of my mountains, looting the beds
    of my creeks,
Them will I take to my bosom, and speak as a mother
    speaks.
I am the land that listens, I am the land that broods ;
Steeped in eternal beauty, crystalline waters and woods.
Long have I waited lonely, shunned as a thing accurst,
Monstrous, moody, pathetic, the last of the lands and
    the first ;
Visioning camp-fires at twilight, sad with a longing
    forlorn,
Feeling my womb o'er-pregnant with the seethe of
    cities unborn.

Wild and wide are my borders, stern as death is my
   sway,
And I wait for the men who will win me—and I will
   not be won in a day ;
And I will not be won by weaklings, subtle, suave, and
   mild,
But by men with the hearts of vikings, and the simple
   faith of a child ;
Desperate, strong and resistless, unthrottled by fear or
   defeat,
Them will I gild with my treasure, them will I glut
   with my meat.

'Lofty I stand from each sister land, patient and wearily
   wise,
With the weight of a world of sadness in my quiet,
   passionless eyes ;
Dreaming alone of a people, dreaming alone of a day,
When men shall not rape my riches, and curse me and
   go away ;
Making a bawd of my bounty, fouling the hand that
   gave—
Till I rise in my wrath and I sweep on their path and
   I stamp them into a grave.
Dreaming of men who will bless me, of women
   esteeming me good,
Of children born in my borders, of radiant motherhood,
Of cities leaping to stature, of fame like a flag unfurled,
As I pour the tide of my riches in the eager lap of the
   world.'

This is the Law of the Yukon, that only the Strong
    shall thrive ;
That surely the Weak shall perish, and only the Fit
    survive.
Dissolute, damned and despairful, crippled and palsied
    and slain,
This is the Will of the Yukon—Lo ! how she makes
    it plain !

197.   *My Madonna*

I HAILED me a woman from the street,
    Shameless, but, oh, so fair !
I bade her sit in the model's seat,
    And I painted her sitting there.

I hid all trace of her heart unclean ;
    I painted a babe at her breast ;
I painted her as she might have been
    If the Worst had been the Best.

She laughed at my picture and went away.
    Then came, with a knowing nod,
A connoisseur, and I heard him say :
    ' 'Tis Mary, the Mother of God.'

So I painted a halo round her hair,
    And I sold her, and took my fee,
And she hangs in the church of Saint Hilaire,
    Where you and all may see.

198. *The Call of the Wild*

HAVE you gazed on naked grandeur, where there 's
    nothing else to gaze on,
Set pieces and drop-curtain scenes galore,
Big mountains heaved to heaven, which the blinding
    sunsets blazon,
Black canyons where the rapids rip and roar ?
Have you swept the visioned valley with the green
    stream streaking through it,
Searched the Vastness for a something you have lost ?
Have you strung your soul to silence ? Then for God's
    sake go and do it ;
Hear the challenge, learn the lesson, pay the cost.

Have you wandered in the wilderness, the sage-brush
    desolation,
The bunch-grass levels where the cattle graze ?
Have you whistled bits of rag-time at the end of all
    creation,
And learned to know the desert's little ways ?
Have you camped upon the foothills, have you galloped
    o'er the ranges,
Have you roamed the arid sun-lands through and
    through ?
Have you chummed up with the mesa ? Do you know
    its moods and changes ?
Then listen to the wild,—it 's calling you.

ROBERT W. SERVICE

Have you known the Great White Silence, not a snow-
    gemmed twig a-quiver ?
(Eternal truths that shame our soothing lies.)
Have you broken trail on snowshoes ? mushed your
    Huskies up the river,
Dared the unknown, led the way, and clutched the
    prize ?
Have you marked the map's void spaces, mingled with
    the mongrel races,
Felt the savage strength of brute in every thew ?
And though grim as hell the worst is, can you round
    it off with curses ?
Then hearken to the wild,—it 's wanting you.

Have you suffered, starved, and triumphed, grovelled
    down, yet grasped at glory,
Grown bigger in the bigness of the whole ?
' Done things ' just for the doing, letting babblers tell
    the story,
Seeing through the nice veneer the naked soul ?
Have you seen God in His splendours, heard the text
    that nature renders
(You'll never hear it in the family pew),
The simple things, the true things, the silent men who
    do things ?
Then listen to the wild,—it 's calling you.

They have cradled you in custom, they have primed
    you with their preaching,
They have soaked you in convention through and
    through ;

They have put you in a showcase ; you're a credit to
    their teaching—
But can't you hear the wild ?—it 's calling you.
Let us probe the silent places, let us seek what luck
    betide us :
Let us journey to a lonely land I know.
There 's a whisper on the night-wind, there 's a star
    agleam to guide us,
And the wild is calling, calling . . . let us go.

199.   *The Mountain and the Lake*

I KNOW a mountain thrilling to the stars,
  Peerless and pure, and pinnacled with snow ;
Glimpsing the golden dawn o'er coral bars,
    Flaunting the vanished sunset's garnet glow ;
Proudly patrician, passionless, serene ;
    Soaring in silvered steeps where cloud-surfs break ;
Virgin and vestal—oh, a very Queen !
    And at her feet there dreams a quiet lake.

My lake adores my mountain—well I know,
    For I have watched it from its dawn-dream start,
Stilling its mirror to her splendid snow,
    Framing her image in its trembling heart ;
Glassing her graciousness of greening wood,
    Kissing her throne, melodiously mad,
Thrilling responsive to her every mood,
    Gloomed with her sadness, gay when she is glad.

ROBERT W. SERVICE

My lake has dreamed and loved since time was born ;
　Will love and dream till time shall cease to be ;
Gazing to her in worship half forlorn,
　Who looks towards the stars and will not see—
My peerless mountain, splendid in her scorn . . .
　Alas ! poor little lake ! Alas ! poor me !

HELENA COLEMAN

200.　　　　　　*On the Trail*

OH, there 's nothing like the prairie
　　When the wind is in your face,
And a thunderstorm is brewing,
　And night comes down apace—
'Tis then you feel the wonder
　And immensity of space !

Far in the gathering darkness
　Against the dying day
The ghostly hills are lying,
　The hills that stand for ay—
How in the dusk they glimmer
　And palpitate away !

　　　.　　.　　.　　.　　.

How vast the world and void !
　No living thing in sight,
As to the lonely prairie
　Comes down the lonely night,
But in your heart what freedom—
　What sense of buoyant flight !

HELENA COLEMAN

Once more the pulses quicken
　　With life's exultant pride,
With hope and high ambition,
　　As on and on you ride,
Till all the old desires
　　Come galloping beside!

Oh, there's nothing like the prairie
　　When the wind is in your face,
And the boom of distant thunder
　　Comes rolling up apace—
'Tis then you feel the wonder
　　And immensity of space!

MARJORIE L. C. PICKTHALL

201.　　　　*A Mother in Egypt*

'About midnight will I go out into the midst of Egypt. . . . And all the firstborn in the land of Egypt shall die, from the firstborn of Pharaoh that sitteth upon the throne unto the firstborn of the maidservant that is behind the mill.'

IS the noise of grief in the palace over the river
　For this silent one at my side?
There came a hush in the night, and he rose with his
　　hands a-quiver
Like lotus petals adrift on the swing of the tide.
O small cold hands, the day groweth old for sleeping.
O small still feet, rise up, for the hour is late.
Rise up, my son, for I hear them mourning and weeping
In the temple down by the gate.

MARJORIE L. C. PICKTHALL

Hushed is the face that was wont to brighten with
laughter
When I sang at the mill ;
And silence unbroken shall greet the sorrowful dawns
hereafter,
The house shall be still.
Voice after voice takes up the burden of wailing,—
Do you heed, do you hear ?—in the high-priests' house
by the wall :
But mine is the grief, and their sorrow is all unavailing.
Will he wake at their call ?

Something I saw of the broad dim wings half-folding
The passionless brow.
Something I saw of the sword the shadowy hands were
holding,—
What matters it now ?
I held you close, dear face, as I knelt and hearkened
To the wind that cried last night like a soul in sin,
When the broad bright stars dropped down and the
soft sky darkened,
And the Presence moved therein.

I have heard men speak in the market-place of the city,
Low-voiced, in a breath,
Of a God who is stronger than ours, and who knows
not changing nor pity,
Whose anger is death.

MARJORIE L. C. PICKTHALL

Nothing I know of the lords of the outland races,
But Amun is gentle and Hathor the mother is mild,
And who would descend from the light of the Peaceful
    Places
To war on a child ?

Yet here he lies, with a scarlet pomegranate petal
Blown down on his cheek.
The slow sun sinks to the sand like a shield of some
    burnished metal,
But he does not speak.
I have called, I have sung, but he neither will hear
    nor waken ;
So lightly, so whitely he lies in the curve of my arm,
Like a feather let fall from the bird that the arrow
    hath taken,—
Who can see him, and harm ?

' The swallow flies home to her sleep in the eaves of
    the altar
And the crane to her nest,'—
So do we sing o'er the mill, and why, ah, why should
    I falter
Since he goes to his rest ?
Does he play in their flowers as he played among these
    with his mother ?
Do the Gods smile downward and love him and give
    him their care ?
Guard him well, O ye Gods, till I come, lest the wrath
    of that Other
Should reach to him there.

MARJORIE L. C. PICKTHALL

202. *Evening*

WHEN the white iris folds the drowsing bee,
    When the first cricket wakes
The fairy hosts of his enchanted brakes,
When the white moth has sought the lilac tree,
And the young stars like jasmine of the skies
Are opening on the silence, Lord, there lies
Dew on Thy rose and dream upon mine eyes.

Lovely the day, when life is robed in splendour,
Walking the ways of God and strong with wine,
But the pale eve is wonderful and tender,
And night is more divine.
Fold my faint olives from their shimmering plain,
O shadows of sweet darkness fringed with rain.
Give me to night again.

Give me to day no more.   I have bethought me
Silence is more than laughter, sleep than tears :
Sleep like a lover faithfully hath sought me
Down the enduring years.
Where stray the first white fatlings of the fold,
Where the Lent-lily droops her earlier gold,
Sleep waits me as of old.

Grant me sweet sleep, for light is unavailing
When patient eyes grow weary of the day.
Young lambs creep close, and tender wings are failing,
And I grow tired as they.
Light as the long wave leaves the lonely shore,
Our boughs have lost the bloom that morning bore.
Give me to day no more.

MARJORIE L. C. PICKTHALL

203.   *Swallow Song*

O LITTLE hearts, beat home, beat home,
   Here is no place to rest ;
Night darkens on the falling foam
   And on the fading west.
O little wings, beat home, beat home,
Love may no longer roam.

Oh, Love has touched the fields of wheat,
   And Love has crowned the corn,
And we must follow Love's white feet
   Through all the ways of morn :
Through all the silver roads of air
We pass and have no care.

The silver roads of Love are wide,
O winds that turn, O stars that guide.
Sweet are the ways that Love hath trod
Through the clear skies that reach to God,
But in the cliff-grass Love builds deep
A place where wandering wings may sleep.

204.   *The Bridegroom of Cana*

VEIL thine eyes, O beloved, my spouse,
   Turn them away,
Lest in their light my life withdrawn
Dies as a star, as a star in the day,
As a dream in the dawn.
   290

MARJORIE L. C PICKTHALL

Slenderly hang the olive leaves
Sighing apart :
The rose and silver doves in the eaves
With a murmur of music bind our house.
Honey and wine in thy words are stored,
Thy lips are bright as the edge of a sword
That hath found my heart,
That hath found my heart.

Sweet, I have waked from a dream of thee,
And of Him,
He Who came when the songs were done.
From the net of thy smiles my heart went free,
And the golden lure of thy love grew dim.
I turned to them asking, ' Who is He,
Royal and sad, who comes to the feast,
And sits Him down in the place of the least ? '
And they said, ' He is Jesus, the carpenter's son.'

Hear how my harp on a single string
Murmurs of love.
Down in the fields the thrushes sing
And the lark is lost in the light above,
Lost in the infinite glowing whole
As I in thy soul,
As I in thy soul.

Love, I am fain for thy glowing grace
As the pool for the star, as the rain for the rill.
Turn to me, trust to me, mirror me,

As the star in the pool, as the cloud in the sea.
Love, I looked awhile in His face
And was still.

The shaft of the dawn strikes clear and sharp.
Hush, my harp.
Hush, my harp, for the day is begun,
And the lifting, shimmering flight of the swallow
Breaks in a curve on the brink of morn,
Over the sycamores, over the corn.
Cling to me, cleave to me, prison me,
As the mote in the flame, as the shell in the sea,
For the winds of the dawn say, ' Follow, follow
Jesus Bar-Joseph, the carpenter's son.'

205.   *Jasper's Song*

WHO goes down through the slim green sallows,
       Soon, so soon ?
Dawn is hard on the heels of the moon,
And never a lily the day-star knows
Is white, so white as the one who goes
Armed and shod where the hyacinths darken.
Then hark, O harken
And rouse the moths from the deep rose-mallows,
Call the wild hares down from the fallows,
Gather the silk of the young sea-poppies, the bloom of
       the thistle, the bells of the foam.

MARJORIE L. C. PICKTHALL

Bind them all with a brown owl's feather,
Snare the winds in a golden tether,
Chase the clouds from the gipsy's weather,
And follow, O follow the white Spring home.

Who goes past with the wind that chilled us,
Late, so late ?
Fortune leans on the farmer's gate,
Watching the red sun low in the south,
With a plume in his cap and a rose at his mouth.
But oh, for the folk who were free and merry
There 's never so much as a red rose berry.
But old earth 's warm as the wind that filled us,
And the fox and the little grey mouse shall build us
Walls of the sweet green gloom of the cedar, a roof
     of bracken, a curtain of whin.
One more rouse ere the bowl reposes
Low in the dust of our lost red roses,
One more song ere the cold night closes,
And welcome, oh welcome, the dark death in.

206.   *The Shepherd Boy*

WHEN the red moon hangs over the fold,
  And the cypress shadow is rimmed with gold,
O little sheep, I have laid me low,
My face against the old earth's face,
Where one by one the white moths go,
And the brown bee has his sleeping place,

293

MARJORIE L. C. PICKTHALL

And then- I have whispered, ' Mother, hear,
For the owls are awake and the night is near,
And whether I lay me near or far,
No lips shall kiss me,
No eye shall miss me,
Saving the eye of a cold white star.'

And the old brown woman answers mild,
' Rest you safe on my heart, O child :
Many a shepherd, many a king,
I fold them safe from their sorrowing.
Gwenever's heart is bound with dust,
Tristram dreams of the dappled doe,
But the bugle moulders, the blade is rust ;
Stilled are the trumpets of Jericho,
And the tired men sleep by the walls of Troy.
Little and lonely,
Knowing me only,
Shall I not comfort you, shepherd boy ? '

When the wind wakes in the apple tree,
And the shy hare feeds on the wild fern stem,
I say my prayers to the Trinity,
The prayers that are three and the charms that are
        seven,
To the angels guarding the towers of heaven ;
And I lay my head on her raiment's hem,
Where the young grass darkens the strawberry star,
Where the iris buds and the bellworts are.
All night I hear her breath go by,
Under the arch of the empty sky ;

MARJORIE L. C. PICKTHALL

All night her heart beats under my head,
And I lie as still as the ancient dead,
Warm as the young lambs there with the sheep.
I and no other,
Close to my Mother,
Fold her hands in my hands and sleep.

ARTHUR L. PHELPS

207.   *Day*

SEA song and wind song,
  Meadows that lie
Tinted half like the sea,
  Half like the sky.

This till the conjuror,
  Far, far away,
Conjuring, sudden brings
  Red from the grey.

Then mark ye magic work—
  Here at my feet,
Wind-flowers look up again,
  Fair faces sweet.

And round the crag's grey top
  Sea-birds in sun—
Light on the pearly wings !
  Day is begun !

PETER McARTHUR

208. *Aspiration*

HOW should I be the master of my ways ?
    When every nerve is vibrant to the sweep
Of dreams that fill the measure of my days,
    Too rare to lose and past all power to keep.
How should I know what it were well to do ?
    When every path has its alluring strain,
Each towering crest its world-revealing view
    Of realms for him who has the will to reign.

And while I waver, lo ! this earthly shard,
    Wherein is breathed the swift compelling fire,
Breaks with the ardour it was shaped to guard ;
    Yet, ever striving, dream-led, I aspire,
Ere all be spent, with reverent hands to light
A guiding star on some hope-kindling height.

W. J. ARMITAGE

209. *Love*

LOVE doth rule each human heart,
    All earth's empires feel his sway ;
Nought mortal can escape his dart,
    Nor rank nor beauty say him nay.

Love, life's sun, doth flame the soul,
    Even to cowards doth courage give,
Drives out all wintry dearth and dole,
    And bids life joyously to live.

295

W. J. ARMITAGE

But love, divine, which ever lasts,
   Draws all its being, strength, and stay,
From that eternal faith which casts
   All doubts, all dreads, and death away.

MARGERY BERRIDGE GREY

210.   *To a Skylark*

WHEN with crimson tints and rare
   Phoebus paints the world so fair,
Then, thou morning minstrel, rise ;
Flood with melody the skies !

When the dawn's gates ope again,
Swell thy tuneful throat ! oh ! then
Serenade the silver stars,
Peeping through the morn's pale bars.

When the azure mists of night
Flee before the morning light,
Pour forth harmony above,
And softly wake my sleeping love !

THEODORE ROBERTS

211.   *The Reckoning*

YE who reckon with England—
   Ye who sweep the seas
Of the flag that Rodney nailed aloft
And Nelson flung to the breeze—

Count well your ships and your men,
　　Count well your horse and your guns,
For they who reckon with England
　　Must reckon with England's sons.

Ye who would challenge England—
　　Ye who would break the might
Of the little isle in the foggy sea
　　And the lion-heart in the fight—
Count well your horse and your swords,
　　Weigh well your valour and guns,
For they who would ride against England
　　Must sabre her million sons.

Ye who would roll to warfare
　　Your hordes of peasants and slaves,
To crush the pride of an empire
　　And sink her fame in the waves—
Test well your blood and your mettle,
　　Count well your troops and your guns,
For they who battle with England
　　Must war with a Mother's sons.

212.　　　*Epitaph for a Voyageur*

CHANGE was his mistress, Chance his counsellor.
　　Love could not keep him.　Duty forged no chain.
The wide seas and the mountains called to him,
　　The grey dawns saw his camp-fires in the rain.

THEODORE ROBERTS

Sweet hands might tremble—Ay, but he must go.
  Revel might hold him for a little space,
But turning, past the laughter and the lamps,
  His eyes must ever catch the luring face.

Dear lips might question ! Yea, and ask again.
  Rare lips, aquiver silently implore,
But ever he must turn his furtive head,
  And hear the other summons at the door.

Change was his mistress, Chance his counsellor,
  The dark firs knew his whistle up the trail.
Why tarries he to-day ?—and yesternight
  Adventure lit her stars without avail !

ALBERT E. S. SMYTHE

213.   *Anastasis*

W HAT shall it profit a man
    To gain the world—if he can—
And lose his soul, as they say
In their uninstructed way ?

The whole of the world in gain ;
The whole of your soul ! Too vain
You judge yourself in the cost.
'Tis you—not your soul—is lost.

Your soul ! If you only knew—
You would reach to the Heaven's blue,
To the heartmost centre sink,
Ere you severed the silver link,

To be lost in your petty lust
And scattered in cosmic dust.
For your soul is a Shining Star
Where the Throne and the Angels are.

And after a thousand years,
With the salve of his bottled tears,
Your soul shall gather again
From the dust of a world of pain

The frame of a slave set free—
The man that you ought to be,
The man you may be to-night
If you turn to the Valley of Light.

214. *The Seasons of the Gods*

I SAT with May upon a midnight hill
   Wrapped in a dusk of unremembered years
   And thought on buried April—on the tears
And shrouds of March, and Youth's dead daffodil

All withered on a mound of Spring. And still
   The earth moved sweetly in her sleep, the Spheres
   Wrought peace about her path, and for her ears
Chimed the high music of their blended will.

ALBERT E. S. SMYTHE

The God who dreamed the Earth, as I this frame
  That makes me thrall to death and coward of birth—
  Dreamed He not March below some vanished Moon—
Under an earlier Heaven's auroral flame
    The cosmic April flowering into mirth
    Of May and joy of Universal June ?

ALAN SULLIVAN

215.   *Suppliant*

GRANT me, dear Lord, the alchemy of toil,
  Clean days of labour, dreamless nights of rest,
And that which shall my weariness assoil,
  The Sanctuary of one beloved breast ;

Laughter of children, hope and thankful tears,
  Knowledge to yield, with valour to defend
A faith immutable, and steadfast years
  That move unvexed to their mysterious end.

216.   *Came Those who Saw*

CAME those who saw and loved her,
  She was so fair to see !
No whit their homage moved her,
  So proud she was, so free ;
But, ah, her soul was turning
With strange and mystic yearning,
With some divine discerning,
  Beyond them all—to me.

ALAN SULLIVAN

As light to lids that quiver
  Throughout a night forlorn,
She came—a royal giver—
  My temple to adorn ;
And my soul rose to meet her,
To welcome her, to greet her,
To name, proclaim, her sweeter
  And dearer than the morn.

For her most rare devising
  Was mixed no common clay,
Nor earthly form, disguising
  Its frailty for a day :
But sun and shadow blended
And fire and love descended
In one creation splendid
  Nor less superb than they.

. . . . . .

You, of the finer moulding—
  You, of the clearer light—
Whose spirit-life, unfolding,
  Illumined my spirit's night,
Stoop not to end my dreaming,
To stain the vision gleaming,
Or mar that glory, seeming
  Too high for touch or sight.

ALAN SULLIVAN

217.   *The Poet Calls*

FILL me with fire and rapture ! Gird me with
      speech divine
   That the word of my mouth be music, that the
   chord of my speech be wine ;
For the soul that trembles within me would marvellous
   things unfold,
   Tho' the world is weary of singing and the eyes of
   the world are cold.

I am the deathless vision, the voice of memorial years,
   The Prince of the earth's rejoicing, the Prophet and
   Priest of tears !
Have I not tasted rapture, have I not loved and died,
   Mounted the peaks of passion, with you been
   crucified ?

Tears and kisses and laughter, arms in a linked embrace,
   Magical union of body, and glory of magical face :
These—shall I sing of them sweetly ? I know when
   the lovers stray
   In the hush where the cloistered woodland broods
   over the wistful day.

Would you I bring my music ? I'll pipe where the
   toilers go ;
   And through your sweat and labour the strain of
   my song shall flow,
Dulcet sweet for your comfort, winged with a delicate
   fire,
   The shout of a strong heart chanting to the lift of
   the soul's desire. .

ALAN SULLIVAN

Come ! I will lead you softly, through floods that are
    smooth and deep,
  And trailed with shimmering curtain of dream-
    embroidered sleep,
To the dim mysterious portal, where the spirit of
    man may see
  The fold of the veil dividing himself from eternity.

And whether you stay to hearken and drink of my
    healing spring,
  Or turn from the plaint of my tender articulate
    whispering—
Ere ever ye came,—I was ancient ; and after ye pass,—
    I come,
  The voice that shall rise in rapture when the moan
    of the earth is dumb.

HECTOR CHARLESWORTH

218. *Sonnets on the Death of Stevenson*

I

WHEN louder voices throbbed with scorn and
    hate,
Ah, dear, glad, soaring spirit of the sun,
The golden loom, from which thy thought was spun,
Sang on with cheer and gentleness elate,
Seeking to end our war and fierce debate
And make our lives in kindlier courses run,
By aid of that sweet wisdom thou had'st won
From Life the Sphinx, and the veiled juggler, Fate !

HECTOR CHARLESWORTH

This be my hope—when from my halting hand,
My pen has dropped for aye, and in the deep
Of yon still sea of death, I sink to sleep,
If some new light should strike across mine eyes—
If I should wake—I worthy be to rise,
And greet thee, brother, in that other land !

II

The sea was ever in thy dreams ; it stirred,
And lisped and sobbed and thundered in thy heart ;
Its ebb and flow inspired thy soul-spun art ;
And as we linger o'er each living word,
Each thought that soars like some far-flying bird—
We know thy secret was the siren song,
The old, old lure that in the ages long
Thy fellow-seers and fellow-dreamers heard.

And where thou liest in thy mountain tomb,
The sea shall sing thy requiem for aye ;
Shall murmur to thy spirit night and day
The mystery of the ebb and flow of things
That, like the fluttering of countless wings,
Quickened thy rare dream-children in the womb.

III

Oh, well-beloved, thou to whom all men
Were brothers whatsoe'er the tongue they spake,
When thy dark liegemen bore thee through the brake
And laid thee in the tomb beyond the ken

Of Old-World strife, thy spirit said ' Amen ! '
Samoa, jewel of the southern main,
After long torture, shrived thee of thy pain,
God could not make it to thee alien !

There, on the mountain, sleep thou to the end ;
Thy requiem the murmur of the sea,
And song of sea-birds wandr'ing far and free !
If thoughtless hands would rive thee from thy tomb,
The living curse that Shakespeare, dying, penned,
Touch thy despoilers like the breath of doom !

GEORGE A. MACKENZIE

219.   *Magellan*

THERE is no change upon the deep ;
 Each day they see the prospect wide
Of yesterday : the same waves leap :
 The same pale clouds the distance hide,
  Or shaped to mountain-peaks their hopes of land
   deride.

On, and still on, the soft winds bear
 The rocking vessel, and the main
That is so pitiless and so fair,
 Seems like a billowy, boundless plain
  Where one might sail, and sail, and ever sail in vain.

GEORGE A. MACKENZIE

Famine is there with haggard cheek,
  And Fever stares from hollow eyes ;
And sullen murmurs rise, that speak
  Curses on him whose mad emprise
    Has lured men from their homes to die 'neath alien
    skies.

But he, the captain, he is calm :
  His glance compels the mutineer :
In fainting hearts he pours the balm
  Of sympathy and lofty cheer :
    ' Courage, a few more leagues will prove the earth
    a sphere.

' The world *is* round : there is an end :
  We do not vainly toil and roam :
The kiss of wife, the clasp of friend,
  The fountains and the vines of home
    Wait us beyond the cloud, beyond the edge of foam.

220.   *High Tide*

THE salt wave, of the quiet valley fain,
  Has pushed across the sands. The talking
    stream
Is silenced by its passing. Will it gain
Th' untroubled reaches where the lilies dream,
To bask in still content beneath the gleam
Of stormless skies ? No ; it has climbed in vain ;
For even now 'tis falling. I could dream
It breathed a long-drawn utterance of pain.

X 2   307

GEORGE A. MACKENZIE

And thou, my soul, thou dost attain release
From mortal sadness in the fields divine
Where thou art often led ; but it is thine
To stay—how short a time ! below thy peace
  The great world travails, like the moaning sea,
  And calls thee back to share its agony.

WILLIAM T. ALLISON

221.   *The Cry of the Romanticist*

TO-MORROW I shall once again behold
   The bright clear weather after skies of grey,
  Forever through the unaccustomed day
I shall be puissant in the lists of old.

Delay not, therefore, shining day of gold,
  But spring eternal from the fields of night,
  And lift my soul into far seas of light,
And bring me near my perfect love, Isolde.

For in this night of time no more I find
  The fluted dreams, unperishing and high,
The ringing temper of the ancient mind.

Glory is gone, while Love, a wasted thing,
  Looks from dim windows on the passers-by,
And Love, alas ! has lost the heart to sing.

WILLIAM T. ALLISON

222.   *O Amber Day*

O AMBER day amid the autumn gloom,
    With languid lids drooping on eyes of dream,
How many ancient poets in their bloom
    Have sung the strange, sad wonder of thy gleam !

O splendid softness of the iron days,
    Mistress between the haunts of life and death,
The poets of our time entune thy praise,
    And love the sweet nepenthe of thy breath.

And so to them lost in thy purple eyes,
    Come visions of the Vallombrosan groves,
Where flaming dawns, and mellow evening skies,
And falling leaves saw old unhappy loves.

223.   *A Galley Slave of Sidon*

A FAIR-HAIRED slave of Sidon, what to him
    Her dream of empire and her fame ?
Chained to the trireme's oar, defiant, grim,
    He cries his curses on her name.

And what to him her purple pride, her quest
    For new dominions, unknown seas,
And all the untouched wonders of the west,
    And apples of Hesperides ?

Dull his poor eyes to pomp, and dead to dreams
  His withered heart ; his Dacian home
All but forgot ; faint and far-off the screams
  Of his young brood destroyed by Rome.

How can his sullen eyes see past the oar
  That holds him to his daily death?
Can Sidon's prayers for her great quest be more
  To this dull slave than idle breath?

To him the cheers, the tumult on the quay,
  Are hollow echoes on the wind ;
The chiefs of Sidon seek the outer sea,
  Fame lures them far, and Fate is blind.

  .   .   .   .

But Sidon's hopes were doomed, and fickle Fate
  Denied the splendid galley's quest ;
Fate heard the slave's prayer daily hissed in hate,—
  His quest was death, his hope was rest.

ALBERT D. WATSON

224. ˚   *One Consciousness*

ONE consciousness is all that is or evermore can be :
  Are not the billows of the world one all-embrac-
    ing sea?
With The Eternal I am one, and only thus am free.
I rise superior to fate ; I challenge fear, I forfeit ease.
I stand heroic and elate, and strong amid th' eternities !

NEWTON MACTAVISH

225.   *Tempora Mutantur*

THEN by the glass how swift the sand set speed,
  How softly-swift the sand that marked the hour
When Barbara fetched to me the spirit-mead
  And urged me to my solitary bower !

I saw her then ; I held her hand in mine,
  And all was sweet within the wondrous hour
When Barbara raised the ruddy, ardent wine,
  And bade me seek my solitary bower.

And soon we thought to turn the wasted glass,
  As, man and wife, we scorned the fleeting hour,
And drank of happiness—for us, alas !
  Too deep within the sense-seducing bower.

.   .   .   .

Now by the glass how slow the sand sets speed,
  How softly-slow the sand that marks the hour
When I, no Barbara to pledge Love's mead,
  Go heartsick to my solitary bower.

WILLIAM CARMAN ROBERTS

226.   *Inscrutable*

HER gold hair, fallen about her face,
  Made light within that shadowy place,
But on her garments lay the dust
  Of many a vanished race.

Her deep eyes, gazing straight ahead,
  Saw years and days and hours long dead,
While strange gems glimmered at her feet,
  Yellow, and green, and red.

And ever from the shadows came
  Voices to pierce her heart like flame.
The great bats fanned her with their wings,
  The voices called her name.

But yet her look turned not aside
  From the black deep where dreams abide,
Where worlds and pageantries lay dead
  Beneath the viewless tide.

Her elbow on her knee was set,
  Her strong hand propt her chin, and yet
No man might name that look she wore,
  Nor any man forget.

FRANCIS SHERMAN

227.   *The Foreigner*

HE walked by me with open eyes,
  And wondered that I loved it so ;
Above us stretched the grey, grey skies ;
Behind us, foot-prints on the snow.

Before us slept a dark, dark wood.
Hemlocks were there, and little pines
Also ; and solemn cedars stood
In even and uneven lines.

The branches of each silent tree
Bent downward, for the snow's hard weight
Was pressing on them heavily ;
They had not known the sun of late.

. . . . . .

There was no sound (I thought I heard
The axe of some man far away),
There was no sound of bee, or bird,
Or chattering squirrel at its play.

And so he wondered I was glad.
—There was one thing he could not see ;
Beneath the look these dead things had
I saw Spring eyes agaze at me.

228. *A Memory*

YOU are not with me though the Spring is here !
And yet it seemed to me to-day as if the Spring
Were the same one that in an ancient year
Came suddenly upon our wandering.

You must remember all that chanced that day.
Can you forget the shy awaking call
Of the first robin ?—And the foolish way
The squirrel ran along the low stone wall ?

The half-retreating sound of water breaking,
Hushing, falling ; while the pine-laden breeze
Told us the tumult many crows were making
Amid innumerable distant trees ;

313

The certain presence of the birth of things
Around, above, beneath us,—everywhere ;
The soft return of immemorial Springs
Thrilling with life the fragrant forest air ;

All these were with us, then. Can you forget ?
Or must you—even as I—remember well ?
To-day, all these were with me, there,—and yet
They seemed to have some bitter thing to tell ;

They looked with questioning eyes, and seemed to wait
One's doubtful coming whom of old they knew ;
Till, seeing me alone and desolate,
They learned how vain was strong desire of you.

229. *Between the Battles*

LET us bury him here,
    Where the maples are red !
He is dead,
And he died thanking God that he fell with the fall
    of the leaf and the year.

Where the hillside is sheer,
Let it echo our tread
Who he led ;
Let us follow as gladly as ever we followed who never
    knew fear.

Ere he died, they had fled ;
Yet they heard his last cheer
Ringing clear,—
When we lifted him up, he would fain have pursued,
    but grew dizzy instead.

314

FRANCIS SHERMAN

Break his sword and his spear !
Let this last prayer be said
By the bed
We have made underneath the wet wind in the maple
    trees moaning so drear :—

' O Lord God, by the red
Sullen end of the year
That is here,
We beseech Thee to guide us and strengthen our
    swords till his slayers be dead ! '

230.   *Te Deum Laudamus*

I WILL praise God alway for each new year.
  Knowing that it shall be most worthy of
His kindness and His pity and His love
I will wait patient, till, from sphere to sphere,
Across large times and spaces, ringeth clear
The voice of Him who sitteth high above,
Saying, ' Behold ! thou hast had pain enough ;
Come ; for thy Love is waiting for thee here ! '
I know that it must happen as God saith.
I know it well. Yet, also, I know well
That where birds sing and yellow wild-flowers dwell,
Or where some strange new sunset lingereth,
All Earth shall alway of her presence tell
Who liveth not for me this side of death.

WILLIAM E. MARSHALL

231. *To a Mayflower*

HATH the rude laugh of Boreas frighted thee,
  My dainty one, that thou hast sought to hide
Thy loveliness from the young Spring, whose bride
Thou art, and, like a novice, ecstasy
Of life renounce, in this dark monast'ry
Of mossy cells ? Nay, my pale beauty, chide
Me not, that I have mocked thy holy pride
With ardent praises of so rare modesty !
For I am come to claim thee, pretty flower,
As a sweet solace for my lady's eyes,—
That thou—thy vigil past—all in a bower
Of love, may'st blush and bloom in glad surprise ;
Happy, that, unawares, thy worth was known,
And all thy fragrance saved for Love alone.

232. *It Seems but Yesterday*

IT seems but yesterday, that I, a boy,
  Made life a play ;
But yesterday, my little cup of joy
  Was full alway.
But ah, 'twas long ago !
—That yesterday of joy and play—
And yet, it may be so
That part of my eternity
Is playtime's yesterday in me.

316

WILLIAM E. MARSHALL

And yesterday it seems, I, ere I laid
  Me down to sleep,
In simple faith clasped childish hand , and prayed
  The Lord to keep
My soul. But 'tis not so !
—The grave of yesterday is deep—
And yet I feel and know,
That part of my eternity
Is that same faith and prayer in me.

233.   *Sunrise in Summer*

IN yonder lovely vale, sweet trysting-place
  For fairies, Nature sleeps in dreamy calm.
A light, as gentle as ethereal balm,
In misty rapture plays about her face ;
The eager waiting winds forget to sigh,
And from her love-expectant lips inhale
The breath of roses ; and the stars grow pale,
As the red-flushing ardent dawn draws nigh,
With softest step, to steal a tender kiss.
The beauty-dreamer stirs ; the airy way
Is lit with spears of gold, and forward press
In haste the splendid chivalry of day.
  With trumpet and with song the echoes ring :
  All Nature is awake, and greets her King.

W. STEWART WALLACE

234.   *Urbs Condita*

THE city like an exhalation rose,
    Stone upon stone, from misty morn till purple
        even-close . . .
A-many many chimneys towering high belched forth
    their flaming smoke
From fierce-flaught forges deep within the old earth's
    hollow womb,
Whereinto men thrust faces, blazing-bright, to stoke,
And then drew back in gloom :
Forges whence came white and hissing iron gauds
That, plunged in water, writhed and sizzled vapid
    steam ;
Whereon the loud-voiced hammers straightly beat
    their iron lauds,
And sparks flew fast, and died the white-hot gleam . . .
In wide-roofed, barn-like buildings men trucked bales
    of lade
With multitudinous echoing, bumped them down,
    and clattered back
Incessantly.   Briareus plied his trade.

Outside in airy, sunbright streets no lack
Of stalwart stallions hauled their creaking loads,
Stressed harness, laboured bulging thews, struck fire
    from flinty roads.
Men shouted, whips swirled out and cracked, on every
    labouring dray
Rails jangled clangingly, or wood-beams bumped, or
    heavy sandstone lay . . .

And high in air stone-masses swung out to their own
    place,
And brown hands gripped and guided them as down
    they came apace ;
Mortared up, and set four-square to all the winds
    that blew,   .
And girded down by girders strong, and rivet, bolt,
    and screw,
They proudly topped the steepy walls, and climbed
    the fiery sky,
Till passionless they set their brows amid the stars
    on high.

235.   *His Face was Lit*

HIS face was lit with the hope of youth,
    His innocence lived in his heart ;
And the fault, the guilt, the shame, in sooth,
    'Twere right to tell apart.

The son of a landed line, he came
    And stood in the midst of the years ;
' Oh, whose is the fault, the guilt, the shame,
    That a mother is put to tears ?

A girl came up and won his soul,
    Innocent, clean, and pure ;
And the fault, the guilt, the shame, as a whole,
    Belonged to the girl, be sure.

The serpent lives and he will not die,
  For he 's damned to endless life ;
But the fault, the guilt, the shame, I cry,
  Was Hers in the Garden of Strife.

236.   1837

(*Loquitur William Lyon Mackenzie*)

SONS of heathered hills of freedom,
  Rax the Queen's Arms off the wall,
Set your caps, and fill your muskets,
  At the country's call.

Take the mattock from the garden,
  And the hay-fork from the byre,
And shoulder, port, present them
  To the Regimentals' fire.

Set the blazing flag of Freedom
  A-flutter in your van,
And sing the song of brotherhood,
  The brotherhood of man.

Fraternity, equality,
  Be all your glowing song,
As by the farm-house windows
  Your dead men tramp along.

CHARLES A. LAZENBY

237.   *Myself*

STRIVING, I sought *Myself* to find
    Through fluent Time's extended sweep ;
I watched the births of Gods and Men,
    The Sowing that we reap.

I saw the first gigantic Form
    Come forth the blackened Void ;
I heard the Roar of the Falling Years
    And lived in the great Sauroid.

Far-pinnacled on heights of Flame,
    I watched the Suns take fire—
I was the music in the Hand
    That played the Cosmic Lyre.

I moved in the Flux of the flowing Years
    Through Rock, and Plant, and Beast.
I entered into the Son of Man,
    For I saw His Star in the East.

I sped in worship to His shrine,
    That Manger, cradled low ;
With Him I suffered on the Cross,
    And was in Him the Woe.

I rise triumphant from the Dead,
    On every Easter Morn ;
In Ecstasies Nirvana reach,
    And with the Gods am born.

CHARLES A. LAZENBY

Jehovah on His silver Throne,
    Ishvara's boundless Form ;
The Silent Braman in the Heart
    I name, and clothe, and warm.

I am the Word that was with God,
    Before the Birth of Time ;
I am the Portal and the Path,
    The Lowly and Sublime.

I am the end of Finite Things,
    The Infinite in Scope ;
Before the Gods that were, I am,
    I am the prisoned Hope.

By *Me* alone you reach to God,
    You serve not Me and Pelf ;
All Happiness abides in *Me*
    For lo ! I am *Yourself*.

JOHN DANIEL LOGAN

238.   *Renouncement*

I BUILT mine altar on thy Heart :
    Each morn I burned Love's incense there :
And thou the hallowed sacrifice
    Blest with thy dear commemorative eyes.

Now thou art gone into the Night,
And Sorrow sits alone with me :
Her cold, dumb lips she will not ope
    To call thee from the sepulchre of Hope.

JOHN DANIEL LOGAN

The darkened house within is still :
And though I wistful vigil keep,
The winds without cry mournfully
    That thou, alas ! wilt not return to me.

.   .   .   .   .   .

Ah, though the days that are to come
Bring not thy lost form back to me,—
Yet will I for Love's sake arise
    Each morn, and to thine Image sacrifice !

239.   *Heliodore Fled*

O WORLD that turneth as a vane that veers !
    In what pure Isles beyond the sensual sight
Dwells Heliodore, whose presence was the light
Of Life's obscure probationary spheres ?—
We pledged her—fervently—our fairest years ;
But she is fled ; and, like the Eremite,—
Companion of the Caves and black-browed Night,—
We feed on Dust and drink the Cup of Tears.

Is there no bloom upon the empty earth
For us, O World—no other gift of bliss ?
Ah, if of Love there be no second birth,
And for our longing lips no lips to kiss,
Grant us this saving boon,—if nothing more,—
Dear dreams of our first Love—lost Heliodore !

A. F. BRUCE CLARK

240.   *A Water Song*

WHEN the shore recedes like a world thrust off,
      And the wind herds the ripples like sheep aflee,
I ship my oars, and, stretched out, I let
      The water and wind take my boat and me.
              Oh, floating along
              To the water's song
While the wavelets gurgle and ripple and cream,
And the fish curve forth in a watery gleam,
And the kingfisher dives and the white gulls scream,
      And the clouds drift all day long.

Lo, into the sunset-gates of light
      I float in evenings clear and cool,
Where the clouds like water-lilies white
      Seem lolling asleep in a golden pool.
              Oh, floating along
              To the water's song
While the sun sheaths his golden sword in the lake,
And every wave is a burning flake,
And guitars in tremulous tones awake
      And echo the evening long.

And I in those secret places go
      Where the shy, young stars come forth at night,
To see themselves in the lake's deep glass
      When darkness has banished the curious light.
              Oh, floating along
              To the water's song

A. F. BRUCE CLARK

When the lake is a palace of pillared fires,
Or a city of churches with silver spires
Drowned for aeons with cross and choirs
    That still chant all night long.

JOHN HENRY BROWN

241.   *Night*

AN earth-throned queen, she leans with languid grace,
    And fills the round of vision radiantly.
Soft lights and shades the heaven of her face
    Endue with spell-framed hints of mystery.
Her breathing, like the flower-sweet breath of May,
    When summer's light wind-heralds run before,
Gives fragrance unto gardens ; while the day,
    Enamoured, through the cloud-hung Western door,
Peers backward. On her jewelled vest are seen,
    'Mid broidered streams and trees, the homes of men ;
Here jolts a rolling wain through meadows green,
    And kine belated wind through yonder glen.
From out her star-inwoven dusk of hair
A silver crescent gleams divinely fair.

RICHARD SCRACE (*Pseud.*)

242.   *The Foundry*

GOD of Every Day. He knew its pattern—
    Thing of wood and iron, soul and thew,
Hammer, beaten out of stress and battle,
    Growing heavier as I stronger grew.

RICHARD SCRACE (*Pseud.*)

Came the anvil out of Earth's rough workshop,
  Where the giant Motive first had play,
Asking mutely for the hammer-music :
  ' I await thee, God of Every Day.'

Vigil of probationing and failure—
  Vision of achievement and desire—
Virgin metal brought to do my bidding—
  God of Every Day, breathe out the fire !

JOHN KILLICK BATHURST
243.   *Love's Pilgrim*

FAR from thy shrine,
  With sterile plains of weary days between,
Hope whispers ever from the void, unseen,
  Thou still art mine—
When 'mid the stress of life, with thee-ward face,
I make my vows toward thy dwelling-place.

At radiant morn,
  As the new day first slants into mine eyes,
Steal thoughts of that glad dawning of surprise
  When Love was born :
And in that place where night and morning meet,
I cast my life, a love-gift, at thy feet.

Beats the fierce noon
  Of sorrow on my head, while the skies as brass
Roof all the path my daily feet must pass,
  Peace cometh soon :
Prone on the sands of absence, lo, I kiss
Thy hands in thought, and find an oasis.

JOHN KILLICK BATHURST

Cometh the night—
I will my carpet of Remembrance spread,
Till dreary space and absence all are sped
Far from my sight,
And down the corridors of silence deep,
Thy white hand beckons me to thee,—and sleep.

PETER MACLAREN MACDONALD

244.   *Unswerved*

THE silv'ry river runneth silently
   Through em'rald meadow and bird-haunted lea ;
Down, down it ever floweth,—
Or north or south wind bloweth,—
Down to the calling sea.

Though here and there its bed is deep and cool,
It ever riseth from each pleasant pool,
And onward, seaward goeth,—
Or east or west wind bloweth,—
On to the wooing sea.

Contrary winds war with the stream to-day,
And turn the trembling surface-flood away.
But well the old stream knoweth,
In spite of wind it goeth—
All to the waiting sea.

VIRNA SHEARD

245.   *In Solitude*

HE is not desolate whose ship is sailing
   Over the mystery of an unknown sea,
For some great love with faithfulness unfailing
   Will light the stars to bear him company.

Out in the silence of the mountain passes,
   The heart makes peace and liberty its own—
The wind that blows across the scented grasses
   Bringing the balm of sleep—comes not alone.

Beneath the vast illimitable spaces
   Where God has set His jewels in array,
A man may pitch his tent in desert places,
   Yet know that heaven is not so far away.

But in the city—in the lighted city
   Where gilded spires point toward the sky,
And fluttered rags and hunger ask for pity,
   Grey Loneliness in cloth-of-gold, goes by.

ERIC MACKAY YEOMAN

246.   *To a Violet*

O VIOLET ! when I look on thy face,
   And on the lofty loveliness that lies
In the high sweetness of thy fragile grace
   And in the pale blue beauty of thy guise,

ERIC MACKAY YEOMAN

Briefly I mark thy charm and darling worth,
   Thy shape and painting all so delicate ;
And straightway new thoughts lead me from the earth,
   And new-known wisdom holds me separate.
I look upon thy beauty's mystery,
And judge thee fair,—and think no more of thee :
   For, as I hold thee in my caring hand,
   New things of heaven and earth I understand.

ARCHIBALD SULLIVAN

247.   *The Mermaid*

THERE is a Mermaid in the Bay
   And she hath called me forth to sup
To eat the white flesh of the moon
   And drain the tide from out her cup,
Her table is amid the rocks
   And all the day her arms swing free
A-gathering in the threads o' foam
   To weave a supper cloth for me.

There is a Mermaid in the Bay
   And she hath trapped the phantom gulls
And caught the silver fish that dart
   Like coins through the ship-wrecked hulls.
But loud she calls ' What boots a feast
   That shows no cloth whereon to spread
The scarlet sunset of my wine
   The pallid starlight of my bread ? '

ARCHIBALD SULLIVAN

There is a Mermaid in the Bay
And from this golden lip of land
I watch her labouring 'mid the foam
With seaweed hair and pearly hand,
Though all the waves like caravans
Bring silver threads and tapestry,
Each one draws back its merchandise
And seeks the desert of the sea.

There is a Mermaid in the Bay,
But till her supper cloth is done,
Pale fringed with tassels of the dawn
Gold hemmed with threads of summer sun,
God wots I wait her on the land,
Until I hear the seaweeds stir
And know it is His saintly will
I should go forth to sup with her.

J. C. M. DUNCAN

248.   *Winter in Canada*

SPIRIT of winter, breathe thou thro' my song,
  I sing not to upbraid as some have sung,
Nor lift I up the puny pipes of scorn
Against the utterance of thine iron tongue.
I am thy child ; I boast that I was born
Upon thy threshold, and have drunk thy wine,
And in thy wilds been nurtured and made strong,
To match my strength with thine.

330

J. C. M. DUNCAN

Season of quickening joys and sharp delights,
They love thee best who meet thee face to face,
In thine own fields, and on thy channelled heights,
Or on the shining floors of open space
Breast thine assaults, and shun
The shelter'd skirmish for the open raid,
And take into their blood the draughts of sun,
That add a biting lustre to thy blade.

Sternest of all that serve the sun's own moods,
Yet most we love thee when thou dost unfold
Thy majesty in storms that put to rout
The hills and fields and woods ;
When day, like a lost star, is whirled about,
And the old earth rocks and reels,
With the mad skies at its heels,
O then our spirits grow strong as thine grows bold.

Yet art thou rich in days of perfect peace,
And sometimes gentle in thy moods as May ;
Thy mornings rise like mirrors that draw down
Out of the heavens the crystal depths of day,
Day that still gathers light with its decrease,
Till hill, and field, and town,
In all the many colour'd splendours shine,
Wherewith the sun doth pave the path of his decline.

The silver flutes of Summer at thy breath
Grew mute, and the last flower
Took from thy lips the icy kiss of death ;
The roving tides stood still when thou didst set

J. C. M. DUNCAN

Thy foot upon them in an iron hour ;
Thy hungry wolf-winds out of East and North
Glutted themselves, and do not now forget
The feast of plenty in the autumn bower,
Blaring thy martial music they go forth,
Where long the heart of Summer hath lain dead,
And the last song to Autumn's ear was lost ;
A milder music hast thou too, instead.
The many myriad sparkling bells of frost,
That ring their crisp chimes to the passing tread.
And when the sun abandons thee to night
Under the weaving spell of star and moon,
The dews of thy white spirit are shed and spun
Into frore flowers and foliage, steeped in light,
That are before the clear unshadow'd noon,
Regather'd to the garden of the sun.
They know not thee who cannot comprehend
Thy spirit in all its moods of calm and stress,
Not to what purpose all thy strivings tend,
For thou dost minister to the rounded year
In things that lead to blessing and to bless ;
And they who doubt shall understand at length,
Thy vestiture is woven of hope, not fear.
And thy true gifts are life, and joy, and strength.

J. EDGAR MIDDLETON

249.   *Canada*
                 (Song for Dominion Day)

TOPPING the hill, the long white road
     Shimmers in Summer heat.
What shall I find beyond the rise ?
Peace and plenty to glad mine eyes,
     Sorrow, or black Defeat ?

All the way I have come, the grain
     Swayed in the languid air,
Clover blushed in a hundred meads,
Dew-drops shone like the diamond beads
     Fairies are wont to wear.

Even the rain on my well-browned face
     Came but to bless and cheer.
There were song-sparrows whistling gay
All along the celestial way.
     Roses were blooming near.

And far away on the snow-capped seas,
     Where the porpoise rolls and the petrel runs,
The Red Cross snaps in the mounting breeze
     From the low grey ships with the gleamimg guns,
—So I journey on to the distant hill,
And never a foeman bars my will.

Over the rise the way is lost.
     Still can my spirit sing.
Over the rise on the road I fare
Are bobolinks in the sunlit air,
     And swallows upon the wing.

                                        333

J. EDGAR MIDDLETON

Peace and roses will joy my soul,
    And in the opal morn,
Still shall I see the elm-trees fair,
Still shall I see the Summer air
    Swaying the golden corn.

While far away by The Lizard light
    Where the gale-lashed billow in fury runs
The Red Cross snaps in the stormy night
    From the ghostly ships with the ghostly guns.
—The white road over the distant hill
Is mine, for a peaceful journey still.

ALEXANDER L. FRASER

250.   *November*

EACH sapless leaf that lingers here
    Where bare woods mourn
Shall soon upon Wind's silvery bier
    Be gravewards borne.

The bees have left our honey-bowers,
    The birds are fled ;
And 'neath the blight of frost our flowers
    Have fallen—dead !

Yon meadow now, where grass grew green,
    No grazing yields :
No bells are heard, no flocks are seen
    In far, fenced fields.

334

ALEXANDER L. FRASER

Where children played till all the ground
    Was wet with dew,
Autumn, to-day, with threatening sound
    Snow trumpets blew.
Fear not November's challenge bold—
    We've books and friends ;
And hearths that never can grow cold :
    These make amends !

251.   *A Gloaming Call*

SOMETIMES at close of day
   As children leave their play,
And dusk dips into dark ;
When winds sweet-scented blow
Up from the past, for voices dear I hark ;
Then this comes soft and low :
' Come in my child ; for quenched is day's last spark.'
Once more my feet those dewy fields do roam,
And through the gloaming shines the light of Home !

INDEX OF AUTHORS

References are to numbers of poems.

INDEX OF AUTHORS

INDEX OF FIRST LINES

INDEX OF FIRST LINES

Oxford : Frederick Hall, Printer to the University